A Second Coming

A Second Coming

A Sad and Twisted Saga of an American Church

Eric D. Johnson

Copyright © 2022 by Eric Johnson.

ISBN Soft Cover: 9780578345215
ISBN eBook: 9780578345222

All rights reserved. No part of this book may be reproduced or transmitted in any form or by any means, electronic or mechanical, including photocopying, recording, or by any information storage and retrieval system, without permission in writing from the copyright owner.

This is a work of fiction. Names, characters, places, and incidents either are the product of the author's imagination or are used fictitiously, and any resemblance to any actual persons, living or dead, events, or locales is entirely coincidental.

Any people depicted in stock imagery are models, and such images are being used for illustrative purposes only
This book was printed in the United States of America.

Rev. date: 05/01/2022

To order additional copies of this book contact:
Magna Libre, Inc.
www. Onyoumark.com

Dedication

Dedicated to "The Black Church". Unrivaled in her commitment to serving the people of God.

Also dedicated to my granddaughter Gia Simone Johnson who was born just as I was finishing this book, and her loving parents, grandmothers, uncles, aunties, and cousins who shared in the joy of her arrival.

Prologue

Folks on the street used to say, "If you weren't at St. Stephens African Baptist on Sunday morning, then you were not really at church." That was back when you could fall out of the club at 2 in the morning, go home and get just enough sleep so that you could get yourself to the church in time for the fashion show and concert taking place at St. Steve's. That is not to say that you couldn't meet God at another church, but back then people were not as concerned about meeting God as they were about meeting that special person of romantic, business, or social interest. Nor could anyone claim that you could not get a good word from the pulpit, quite the contrary, but for many of her congregants not even God could penetrate the prior evening's onslaught of liquor and adulterous conversation. For most people, God had ceased to be the point, and that was the problem.

The old folks, for whom God most certainly <u>was</u> the point, carried the church back then. The deacons were old, venerable men who mortgaged their houses to pay the church's note and built a church annex so that their grandbabies would have a place to go to Sunday school. Old St. Stephens had a Mother's Board filled with spiritual women who knew how to get a prayer up, and when things were financially bleak, knew how to go into their bosoms and produce the exact amount of cash to get you out of your last jam and into the next.

Then there was the magical quality of the building itself. The unique architecture of St. Stephens made her stand out like a pearl on black velvet. Unlike modern prefab churches, where the sanctuary could double as a furniture warehouse, St. Stephens was majestic. You could pick her up and set her down on Holy Corner in Edinburgh, and she would fit right in, rubbing her gothic elbows with those of her Scottish neighbors. The church was adorned with stained glass windows extolling the Gospel story and her rich history that began at the end of the eighteenth century. Angelic depictions were etched into the skylight that overhung the Narthex, casting holy images upon all who entered the sanctuary. A huge stained-glass image of Christ rose above the altar, looking plaintively into the congregation, beseeching them to come unto Him, and lay their burdens at His feet.

St. Stephens was abundant in generosity, glorious in worship, and rich in spirit. It could be said that this body of Christ altered the arc of the community, vaulting its people above moral desolation, poverty, and despair, into the warm slipstream of Christian love and comfort.

The spirit of the Church was tied to the work of Reverend Hugo "Papa Bear" Bearman, Sr. He was a rotund jovial man, who looked and acted like everyone's lovable grandfather. Hospital patients were heartened when the elf-like presence of Papa Bear Bearman poked his balding head into their room and asked with a gravelly voice, "How're you doing Sugar-Babe?" He called everyone Sugar-Babe: man, woman, and child. He was that kind of man, loving and familiar.

Bearman would press in close to a man while placing one warm hand on the man's shoulder and ask, "How are you doing Babe?" The man would drop all masculine pretenses and respond with a look that said, "My life is a straight-up mess." To which the small round man would say, "Come with me brother. Let's talk." Then he'd just listen to the man with quiet concern, not filling the air with self-righteous advice but dignifying him with a quietness that spoke volumes.

St. Stephens stood tall and silent, an elegant rock in a weary land. The community evolved around her, but the church never changed, oblivious to the truth that even rocks erode. St. Stephens was out of step with a world where sex predators published books on family values, adults married people they had never met, and adolescents advised on parenting. The church played host to more funerals than weddings and celebrated more retirements than baby blessings. The staff, noting the shrinking congregation, and diminished offerings, tried in vain to get Rev. Bearman to adopt modern methods of communication: social media, streaming of services, and podcasts, but old Papa Bear just smiled genially and said something mystical like, "Don't worry about that Shug. The Lord will take care of it."

If Reverend Bearman had a flaw it was that he could never contemplate the end of things. His wife complained that he didn't know how to end a sermon. His son complained that he didn't know how to end a conversation. After staff meetings, which he always ended with a rambling discourse, his staff would gather at a local tavern and chant mockingly:

"As it was in the beginning, is now, and ever shall be, words without end…"

He feared endings, which to him produced only nostalgia and regret, but as any bartender at closing time will tell you, "All good things must come to an end."

Endings can be unexpected, untimely, and inevitable, and all three of these apocalyptic horsemen rode into St. Stephens one Sunday morning early in the year when days are short, cold, and dark.

Reverend Bearman sat in his study contemplating a series of sermons that would take the congregation through the Lenten season and culminate during Holy Week. It occurred to him that once the New Year started, there was no going back to the prior year. Your victories and defeats, hopes and fears were all in the past. The new year lay in front of you, empty and vast with opportunities and potential. The future was here and there was no turning back. He liked the feel of that phrase, "No Turning Back." He closed his eyes and let the Spirit reveal verses and hymns to support his thesis, but nothing came. Nothing of substance anyway, just bits of a contemporary gospel song --- *"Can't go back, won't go back, to the way it used to be."*

His mind wandered to the old theory that people who died and saw heaven would not return to this world even if they could. He wondered if that were true. Was heaven so magnificent that having experienced it for a second would wipe away your memory of love and life? *"Can't go back, won't go back, to the way it used to be."*

Having nothing else to use as a message, he decided to go with it: "No Turning Back". He asked the music director to play William McDowell's contemporary gospel song, which he recalled went something like:

I've been changed, healed, freed, delivered
Right now is the Moment
Today is the Day
I've been changed

As the choir sang, the people stood praising and worshiping, and Reverend Bearman slowly moved toward the pulpit, raised his hands, not to quiet the people but to praise his God, and in his distinctive baritone, uttered the title of his sermon,

"No turning back"

"No turning back, my friends."

"No turning back…"

He fell to his knees as though in prayer, his arms outstretched toward heaven. The congregation shouted, "Yes," but then a strange rumbling murmur rippled through the assembly.

The old man rolled clumsily to his side, clutching the microphone to his mouth, allowing the congregation to hear his final groan.

1

Man on a String

Sunday Morning– One week before the second coming.

The Reverend Dr. Ronald Barbados sat at his desk eyeing a plate of rapidly cooling eggs, hash browned potatoes, and bacon. The bacon was so crisp and lean that it could make a hungry man weep with anticipation. Barbados discretely licked his lips and moved fitfully in his chair, glancing down at his breakfast while attempting to appear composed and self-contained, a man far too preoccupied with the affairs of humanity to indulge in something as mundane as breakfast.

Barbados had been taught by his mother, an aristocratic woman of impeccable manners, that it was impolite for a man to eat in the presence of a guest who had not been served, but he couldn't help imagining himself forking up piles of soft creamy eggs with just the right portion of spicy potato, topping it all off with a half strip of crisp bacon. He could smell the aroma of peppers and onions as they all but sang praises to God. "That's why some brothers hum when they eat," Barbados thought. "They hear the harmony drift up from a well-cooked meal, and they just join in, humming as they devour the choir."

He only had a few minutes before he was expected in the sanctuary, but his mother's affected tone yammered inside his brain, "Sit up Roland darling, and rest your fork until your guests have been served." He doubted that the three women arrayed before him knew enough etiquette to warrant his caring, but he couldn't shake his mother's subconscious badgering.

Celestine Nash sat at the center of the trio looking imperious and impatient, her eyes radiating Afro-Asian beauty, her long legs crossed at the knee with one stiletto shod foot bobbing hypnotically up and down. Barbados tracked her gaze as she glanced at his breakfast, shifted to his lips, and made deadly contact with his eyes.

"Can I get them to bring you and the other ladies a plate Sister Nash?" he asked, trying to break the spell and appear cordial over the audible groan of his stomach.

"No. I'm vegan. You *know* that" she said.

"Really?" He laughed. "What is vegan exactly, some kind of vegetarian?"

She watched him stoically.

"Can I get any of you a cup of tea then, organic decaf?"

She waited several seconds before responding, during which Barbados wondered if vegans could drink tea. He chanced another look into her hazel eyes, which on any other woman would be beautiful, but on her seemed carnivorous and wolf-like.

"No. I've not come for breakfast. Not for *that* greasy mess," she pointed an accusatory finger at his eggs, which were becoming too cold and dry to be slandered for greasiness. "I have a few concerns which I'd like to discuss with you before you go out there." She waved in the general direction of the sanctuary.

Barbados leaned forward as if to go for his fork, remembered his manners, and quickly folded his hands awkwardly in his lap.

"Concerns? Like what?"

Celestine Nash held one immaculately manicured hand up like a traffic cop signaling Barbados to stop talking. He looked down at the eggs congealing on his plate, wondering if they were still edible.

Celestine responded in the same irritatingly proper tone of voice his mother used, "Nothing earth-shattering Ronald, it's just that I need you to emphasize our upcoming *Women of Power Prayer Conference* during your homily."

"I can work that in," said Barbados.

"No, Ronald, I don't want you working *anything in,*" she replied while rolling her eyes and exchanging looks of disgust with her colleagues. "I need to make sure you have the facts at hand."

"I know the facts, Celestine. The conference is …" Barbados looked down at his desk calendar searching in vain for the conference entry.

"Don't bother Ronald," said Celestine. "We've written something out for you."

Celestine placed a laminated set of Day-Glo pink index cards on Barbados's desk and pushed the deck toward him with one teal fingernail.

Barbados flipped through what felt like a dozen cards, each filled with typed text.

"Celestine, you've given me ten minutes to deliver my message. Ten minutes Celestine. Barely enough time to raise a text. And now you want me to stand up there and read from these cards. I'll get more people to your conference if you just let me do what I do."

"What *you do,* Ronald is stand up there whooping and shouting, and sweating like a Georgia field hand."

"That's called preaching," said Barbados.

"Whatever you call it," Celestine replied, "It's crass and crude. You don't see Joel Osteen hooting and hollering like that."

"Crude?" Asked Barbados. "Osteen is not part of our tradition. We've discussed this."

"Tradition," said Celestine, managing to sound disappointed and irritated at the same time. "That's the problem Ronald. Your style of preaching is no longer effective with our demographic. It just isn't. We have the metrics to prove it. I can have Teeny review them with you – *again* – or you can trust us and read from the prepared script."

Barbados looked at Teeny – a short pugnacious looking woman who, ungraciously, reminded him of a pit bull. He decided it was better to deal with the index cards he was dealt.

Barbados read the first sentence silently, "Our mission is to **leverage** the praying power of women in a **synergistic** exercise of mutual accountability as we **harmonize** in prayer."

He looked up at Celestine who arched a menacing eyebrow in his direction.

"Celestine, I'm not sure what you are really trying to say. Why some words in bold italics and other words are underlined?

"We want you to emphasize the bold words," Celestine replied.

"What about the underlined words?" Barbados asked.

"You should *really* emphasize those," interjected Teeny in a deep raspy voice, "It's called oratory."

"Every other word is emphasized," laughed Barbados. "I'll sound like a lunatic."

"Yes, well isn't that what preachers in your little *tradition* are supposed to sound like?" Asked Celestine. "Teeny wrote this to match your style. I think it's brilliant."

"Teeny wrote this?" Asked Barbados, stealing a glance at Teeny who appeared to be flexing her pectoral muscles.

"Teeny needs to stay off the steroids. I would never use words like synergize and leverage in the same freaking sentence."

"Nevertheless, we need to hear you read it aloud," said Celestine as she leaned forward allowing her black and white checked skirt, which was already short and tight, to rise higher up her thighs.

"You need to have your brain examined," said Barbados, who broke form and shoveled a forkful of cold eggs into his mouth.

"I need to hear from you, Ronald. It will sound so good when you read it."

The bobbing stiletto gave rise to thoughts that Barbados did not want to entertain when he was being called upon to preach.

Using her pouting teenager voice, Celestine said, "I want you to recite it in front of me, Ronald. I want to know that you'll get it right."

Barbados had studied Greek in Greece and Hebrew in Israel. He had won the Homiletics Award at Princeton Seminary and written numerous articles for *Christianity Today*. He had an undergraduate degree in contemporary English literature from Columbia and had spent years sitting at the feet of his Father and Grandfather, both legendary men of God. Yet this woman, with her associate's degree in—what was it—marketing, *needed* to hear him read aloud. Yet, the skirt, the subtle design of her stockings, the bobbing stiletto mingled with the taste of cold eggs to quell his outrage and dampen his resolve.

Celestine once again held her hand up, and with a smooth wave summoned Janice McRae, a tall dark-skinned woman with flowing blond hair, to take away his breakfast.

"He's let it get cold," said Celestine, "and we really need to go over his sermon."

Barbados looked at the typed copy, squeezed a single space onto the small cards. He looked over at Teeny, sitting there with her elbows resting on her knees, holding her head in her thick hands, staring at him like he was an elaborately costumed puppet. He began reading aloud, and with each utterance, he felt less like a minister and more like a marionette.

2

The Host

Sweat peppered Barbados's forehead as he read the phrases "Spiritual bandwidth" and "Neo-modern family." He lost his Ivy League mojo when he got to the words "Sanctified unanimity," and stabbed his forefinger in the air as he pronounced each syllable.

Teeny, misreading his sarcasm for enthusiasm, leaped from her chair growling "Truth!" While pounding her fist into the palm of her hand. She mumbled something about Tupac Shakur, whose tattooed countenance leered from her left bicep.

Celestine asked him to stop reading so that she could huddle with Janice and Teeny at his small oval worktable. They read bits of the script aloud, each woman pantomiming her imitation of a Black preacher.

"I used to be the Senior Pastor," he thought as he watched Janice toy with the ends of her blond hair and Teeny gnaw at her chipped, poorly painted fingernails. "I was the Man, the Head Negro in Charge of one of the largest Black congregations in the United States. And I had a fine wife, God rest her soul. Times like this I wish I had died with her. She used to ride my nerves about how I needed to watch out for Celestine – how she was an ice-cold bitch who would destroy my ministry. Now that she's gone, I see her point; isn't that always the way. Damn, here I am trapped in a scene straight out of Miles Davis Bitches Brew, or Hamlet with the witches stirring up my life like a big cauldron of slop. I've lost my…?" Barbados knew exactly what he had lost, and it was something more valuable to him than his wife of seven years who had died in a zip line disaster.

"I've let these women steal my damn title," he thought, his face burrowed into a spider web of fingers. People work long and hard to acquire the right to be called Doctor or Reverend or Mayor. Titles are a recognition of rank, of service, of accomplishment. Clergy – of all people – do not take titles lightly, maintaining an almost maniacal grip on their various nom de plumes: Father, Reverend, Pastor, Bishop, Elder, Apostle, or Pope. It is drilled into you at your clerical birth to insist on being called by your title.

A year earlier, not long after he had buried his wife, Barbados had vigorously defended his hard-won title of Senior Pastor. He remembered saying, "Celestine, I minister to people, it's not what I do, like some job or function. It's not a career. It is *who* I am. It is who I was *called* to be. I lead people spiritually; I am a Pastor, a leader of God's flock, not a host of some damn show."

He had said this with intensity, and passion, a man of God speaking on behalf of every man or woman of God who had ever taken up the sacred mantle, donned the robe and held the crooked staff. His speech was diminished, only slightly, by his having delivered it while lying naked next to Celestine, their legs intertwined, her fingers caressing his chest. Her reply was seared into his memory:

"Ha, ha."

Those were her exact words, "Ha, and ha."

Celestine was not the type of woman who laughed audibly. No, she slowly and distinctly repeated two words: "Ha", and "ha."

She then added by way of explanation, "If you need to think of yourself as a spiritual leader Ron, then I suppose I cannot stop you. But if each of us is to be our own God, why do we need a spiritual leader?"

"Where did you get the idea that we were to be our own God?" Asked Barbados.

"From you Ron, I learned it from one of your sermons. You said we were a Royal Priesthood, a chosen nation of particular people. I remember because it sounded so wonderful: *Royal Priesthood!*"

"First, its *peculiar* people, not *particular* people, and we're a *holy nation* not a *chosen* nation; that spot is already taken, but the point is we can each be our priest. This means that we can interpret the Bible on our own and pray for our salvation, and for that of others. We believe in the priesthood of believers."

"So, we're not a Royal Priesthood?"

"We are, but it's metaphorical."

"Priests, Nations, Royalty, it's all the same to me," said Celestine. "You overthink things and get so preachy. It's so confusing. Wouldn't it be so much easier if you just *facilitated* a discussion with regular people?"

"Facilitated what discussion?" Asked Barbados.

"Yes!" Responded Celestine, excited that he was finally getting the point. She jumped astride Barbados like she was riding him into battle.

"You know," she added, "Like a co-host on a talk show."

"A co-host?" Replied Barbados who had begun repeating the last word of every sentence Celestine uttered.

"You know, like Jimmy Fallon or Kimmel."

"Kimmel," Barbados rasped.

"Yes, Ron. You would be the *Host* of the Sunday Worship Experience!"

"Experience!" Cried Barbados.

"Yes, you would be the host!" Yelled Celestine as she peered down at Barbados.

"Host!" Yelped Barbados hoarsely.

Barbados couldn't remember how the conversation ended, but the next time he took the pulpit at the CST he did so as the *Host of the Sunday Worship Experience*.

***

Barbados recited the edited version of the announcement under the critical eyes of Celestine Nash and her team. When they were satisfied that he was reading it properly, with the inflections and tone of a skilled voice-over man, the threesome walked out of his office leaving a waft of coconut with hints of orange blossom in their wake. They each glanced knowingly at Barbados as they exited his office.

As the women left, a thin, balding man entered the office, greeted each woman politely, and managed to smile despite having been serially ignored.

Barbados greeted him with a deep laugh and a smothering hug that made the man laugh as he gave Barbados a fatherly pat on the back. The lapel of his dark blue suit was festooned with buttons and pins from long-dead fundraising efforts and ancient church organizations like the men's fellowship and Baptist Youth League which had ceased to exist. The faded badge on his suit pocket read Deacon Rush – St. Stephens African BC. The badge and the lapel buttons were part of a silent protest, an act of defiance symbolizing an era when hard-working black men like Rush were the backbone of the church. Men who would provide money to pay the church's heating bill, and volunteer to drive the Pastor and his wife all over town. He was part of a cohort that shoveled snow in the winter, mowed the church lawn in the summer, and swept up, cooked up, and cleaned up, all because they believed they were servants in the house of God. But like Deacon Rush, his badges, and buttons, these men had become obsolete.

Barbados could hear raucous laughter coming from the waiting room outside of his office, the usual effect that Celestine and her posse had on any group of men.

"That boy is out there cutting up Pas… I mean uh Reverend, I mean, ugh," said Deacon Rush, staring up at the ceiling as he searched in vain for Barbados's correct title.

"Don't worry about it Deak," said Barbados. "Just call me Ron like everyone else around here."

"I can't do that," said Deacon Rush. "No sir! I just can't. Let me close the door and we'll have a word of prayer and get you out there to the waiting congregation."

Barbados could hear a deep booming voice bellowing "Girl you look so good I could sop you up like gravy."

Deacon Rush attempted to close the door and was pushed back into the room like he was wearing roller skates.

"Watch out Deak!" Bearman yelled. "Why are you always trying to keep me from conversing with my Pastor?"

Deacon Rush began to nervously explain, "No, no, he wa wa wa…"

"Shut up Rush," said Bearman, "You always stuttering and stumbling like an old fool. That's why we can't let you pray in public anymore. Take you ten minutes to get out a good Lord have mercy. You be like Lo Lo Looooord… ha have us, Murphy…" As he spoke Bearman staggered around the room in a spastic pantomime of the deacon.

"That's enough Bearman," said Barbados.

Rush lowered his head and began to move toward the door, but Bearman stopped him. "Stay put old man. I got big news; the biggest goddamn news an old man like you has ever heard. Sorry for cussing but this shit is big."

Huguenot "Huggey" Bearman wore a black Stetson and darkly tinted glasses. He claimed to need the hat and the glasses to protect his eyes from the glare of artificial light. He could tolerate natural light, but prolonged exposure to fluorescent light caused migraine headaches which subsided only after he'd become temporarily blind.

"Go ahead then Huggey," said Barbados, making a show of looking at his watch. "Remember, you hit me with a fine the last time I was late for service."

"They can wait," said Bearman. "They're out there singing and clapping. They like the music better than listening to you running the drip lip. And this news is big, it's huge, it's colossal."

"OK," said Barbados, "We're all happy you've been hitting the thesaurus, but could you just tell us what this news is so that we can go out there and do our jobs."

"Job? You hear that Deak? This boy couldn't take a real job if you poured it on him. Standing up there talking to a bunch of self-important buppies. That ain't work."

Bearman popped his cuffs so that just the right amount of fabric and gold cufflink peaked out from the jacket sleeves of his pinstriped suit.

"Well, it's what you pay me to do," said Barbados, a touch of anger showing in his voice.

"Don't catch an attitude on me, Ron. I'm just messing with you. Besides, I got the news that is so big it's gonna just blow your puny little preacher mind."

Bearman took a seat and reached into his breast pocket for a cigar, which he placed into his mouth while patting himself as though looking for his lighter.

"See boys," began Bearman examining the tip of his unlit stogie, it ain't no secret that our numbers are down. I mean we are pulling in the people but the money we are collecting is just enough to make our monthly nut. Like those old preachers used to say, 'Our money is funny, and our change is strange' the big money is escaping us, and we've run out of gimmicks."

"You mean ministries," said Barbados.

"Gimmicks, ministries, whatever you want to call it, our act has gotten stale," replied Bearman. "Or should I say *your* act has gotten stale."

"We kept you here to generate revenue Barbados, and you did alright for a while. The Legacy of Hope scam was inspired, inspired!"

"That was no scam," said Barbados. "We encourage our members to name the church as a beneficiary on their insurance policies. That is completely legal, and you know it."

"Come on Doctor," replied a grinning Bearman. "If you don't think selling term insurance to old folks on the condition that they name us as the beneficiary is a scam then I ain't mad at you. Now, some of their relatives who pay the premiums may get a little ticked after Big Mama goes tits up and they find out they ain't gonna get a dime, but, hey, I'm not mad at you Ron, not me, not me."

Deacon Rush interrupted, "Gentleman, in the interest of time, I think we need to..."

"Shut up Deak," shouted Bearman. "You sure is rude. Now that Deacon, what's his name, the one that doesn't talk, he's my kind of niggah. You never see him or hear him. You gotta love a brother like that."

Bearman took off his tinted eyeglasses revealing tiny red watery eyes, lidless pinpricks, revealing no human emotion. He had no eyebrows or eyelashes, just two tiny pink eyes that were entirely too small for his massive face. He took a tissue from the desk, breathed on each lens of his eyeglasses, and used the tissue to wipe them before replacing them on his face.

"Oh boy," said Bearman chuckling to himself. "This news is so big I could shout." He did a pirouette, like a dancing bear in a pinstripe suit.

Deacon Rush fidgeted nervously. It was his job to pray with Barbados and get him into the sanctuary. The praying part was his idea, but Barbados seemed to like it, and it was what he had always done. But his real job was to get him to the sanctuary on time for the live streaming.

A red light above the door began to flash and a machine-like voice rasped, "2 minutes to air, 2 minutes to air…"

"Whatever it is will have to wait," said Barbados.

"Guess it will, said Bearman. Probably best I don't tell you anyway. You wouldn't be able to keep your shit together if you knew what I knew, and Celestine will kill you if you get distracted and mess up her announcement."

Barbados slid the laminated deck of index cards into the inside breast pocket of his suit jacket and walked purposely toward the sanctuary with his deacon escort in tow.

3

Going Rouge

Barbados could feel the beat coming from the sanctuary long before he heard what they were playing. The rhythm pulsed through his spirit like razor-thin shards of Afrocentric funk. The beat reminded him that he was a man of God, ordained to preach the Gospel in season and out of season. It didn't matter what he was called or what he wore. A little fire began burning on the inside, too powerful to be restrained by notes and cue cards written by supercilious women who were not led by the Spirit.

Yet, even as he began to strut in time with the beat, the words of Huggey Bearman nipped at his subconscious like a thousand rats with huge yellow teeth and red eyes dripping mucus. He wondered what the pompous trustee had up his sleeve, what news was he hiding? The reptilian bastard had used "Good news" to claw his way inside his head.

As he neared the entrance to the sanctuary he was confronted by a slightly overweight woman with a flaming red afro, huge round-framed eyeglasses, and an angry case of acne that spread across her cheeks and forehead.

She rolled her eyes, popped the gum that she was chewing, and said, "He's here," into the mouthpiece attached to her headset.

She yanked a sheet of paper from the overstuffed clipboard sending other sheets and cards drifting toward the floor in a blizzard of disorganization and poor time management.

"Shit," she muttered as she clutched the falling sheets to her chest. She was wearing a low-cut dancer's top which allowed her breasts and stomach to balloon up and out.

"Here," she said, thrusting a sheet of paper at Barbados.

"What's this?" He asked.

"Nash's announcement. You're to read it verbatim. No ad-libbing, no sermonizing, no comments. You're late and we're streaming live." She said all of this in a dull emotionless whisper so as not to be overheard.

"I already have Sister Nash's announcement."

"Changed," she said, preoccupied with whatever was coming through her headset.

"I don't have time to review this."

"You would have had time if you had come out earlier. But you were back there with the old man," she said nodding toward Deacon Rush.

Barbados tolerated her rudeness because he remembered that Deacon Rush was her uncle. Rush had told him that she had been raised in the church, a pleasant child with neat corn-rowed hair, who wore pretty dresses and shiny patent leather shoes. Back then she was Brittany Jackson, a girl who could sing and play the piano and the violin. Now, she was a pushy, sun-struck version of Raggedy Ann who insisted on being called Bee-Jax.

He looked at the paper and saw a crudely redacted version of the text Celestine had provided in his office. Every other word had been blacked out, and edits had been made in the minuscule script, crammed into the margins and in between lines of type. The edits were made with a felt tip pen that had smeared, making most of the words unintelligible.

"I can't read this," said Barbados.

"I can't deal with your drama right now," replied Bee Jax. "You're on in about 10 seconds, so just get over yourself and read it. No ad libbing, no sermonizing, no comments."

"You don't understand", said Barbados. "I cannot make out the words. I don't understand what is on this page, it's a mess."

"Let me see it," said Deacon Rush, clumsily donning his reading glasses as he eyed the paper.

Rush's mouth began to move as he attempted to read the hieroglyphics scribbled on the page. Bee Jax rolled her eyes and looked disdainfully at her uncle.

"This is useless," said Barbados. "I'm reading the text she gave me this morning."

"It's your funeral," said Bee Jax "You're on in 5, 4, 3, 2..."

She pushed Barbados out into the sanctuary as his entry music came up.

The congregation that greeted Barbados looked the same as it always had. Women in bright colored dresses were standing with arms raised, worshiping in the Spirit of the music and dance that were a prelude to the preacher's entrance. Old St. Stephens worshiped the same way, but back then the worship was not a prelude to anything, it was part of the whole fabric of worship which included the sermon, the Lord's Supper, the collection, the announcements, the ushering, and the nursing. Everything flowed from one meaningful experience of God's grace to the next. The experience at The CST looked the same, but something about it felt alien to Barbados.

He sensed that the people were seeking "A Word from the Lord", that they were yearning to find the truth that could transform their lives. Their faces wore expressions of expectation. They were looking for their breakthrough and had come to church needing him to say something that would provide the spark that would ignite their spirits.

The problem was that he wasn't even sure he was standing in front of believers. Huggey had once hired homeless men to pass out flyers to tourists touting visits to the CST where one could "experience the authenticity and passion of the traditional Black church." For all, he knew his audience was peppered with visitors from Germany and France who didn't understand a word he was saying but sure did like the music.

Barbados remembered the old church, with the missionaries seated together dressed in white, the restless children and crying babies, the deacons perched on the front row, eyeing him critically but encouraging him generously with grunts of amen. They were gone now, everyone was gone.

The pulpit was gone as well, forcing Barbados to stand on a spot that was taped to the floor. He was handed a wireless microphone just as a spotlight lit him up.

He looked at the ridiculous mass of scribble that Bee Jax had handed him and placed it in his breast pocket.

***

Celestine Nash eyed him suspiciously while glancing at a neatly typed copy of the script that she expected Barbados to read. She had spent months planning a Women's retreat that was designed to elevate the women of the CST. It would inspire them, uplift them, and exult them. Most of all it would provide the platform for a twenty-minute live-streamed talk show that she knew would go viral.

For reasons that were never clear to Celestine, church women needed everything they did to be affirmed by their Pastor. It was absurd to think that a group of powerful women would need, *really need*, the acquiescence of a man to advance their program and validate their worth. She had attempted to counter this paternalistic absurdity by striking at its heart.

Her first step was to realign the church with a wonderful new – gender-neutral - denomination called The Secular Cathedral Ministries of the USA Inc., not to be confused with Secular Cathedral Ministries of America Inc. The switch from being a traditionally Black Missionary Baptist church to joining The Secular Cathedral Ministries of the USA Inc. was a nasty bit of business that came down to a vote at a church meeting. The vote ended up being 4 in favor, one against, and 149 abstentions which, due to an oddity in the church bylaws, were transferred by proxy to the head of the human resources department who just happened to be Celestine Nash.

Next, Celestine initiated her rebranding campaign. Realizing that for many women the title of Pastor was a coded synonym for "father" or worse, "husband" she received divine inspiration to rename the Pastor "Host of the Sunday Worship Experience".

Now as she sat watching Barbados looking luscious in his impeccably tailored suit, she could almost understand how these women could become enraptured by the one man who treated them like they were special. That was until she saw him take her script, fold it, and slide it into his jacket pocket.

"He's going rouge," she whispered to Janice McRae.

***

"Ah yes," pronounced Barbados, "Yes. That's right. How great *Thou* art. How Great is *Thy* faithfulness"

"That is not in the script," said Teeny. "Is this man going to try to preach?"

"Rise to your feet if you know that we serve a faithful God," preached Barbados.

People rose all over the sanctuary shouting "Amen!".

"Ah yes," said Barbados, now pacing back and forth on the raised altar, forcing the cameramen to follow his movements. "I have an important announcement to read to you, and don't worry Sister Nash, I am going to read it. But the presence of the Lord is here, and I just need to stop..." When he said the word "Stop," he literally stopped walking as if frozen in mid-step. The congregation roared their approval, "and thank God for His presence and for His blessing and for His power, and for His mercy, Ahhhhhh! Sometimes, no matter what you are doing or where you are going you just have to STOP!" Again, he stopped mid-step and froze in place. "And acknowledge the power and grace and mercy of an all-wise God."

Out of the corner of his eye, Barbados saw a small man in a black suit, white shirt and a black tie. Barbados thought he had seen the man before, sitting where the deacons used to sit, but he wasn't sure. The man was staring straight ahead, looking at nothing. Barbados saw the man turn for a second and look at him, they made eye contact, a subtle connection that was so fleeting Barbados could not capture the meaning.

Barbados held his face toward heaven and raised his arms in exultation. The congregation did the same and the place vibrated with joy.

"I really hate when he does this," whispered Janice McRae, pushing her long blond hair away from her ebony face, "it's so fake, so pretentious."

Celestine had no choice but to stand with her arms upraised because, as phony a performance as it was, the people were into it and she could not be caught rooted in her seat like a spiritual killjoy. With her hands raised and her face lifted heavenward, she prayed that God would shut him up.

Barbados was strutting around crying,

"Ahhh yes."

"He's been good, good, he's been so good to me," he sang.

"Ahhh yes, beloved, he's been good, so good, he's been so good to me."

"I don't know about you church, but he woke me up this morning, and he started me on my way.

I'm telling you that He's been good, good, He has been so good to me."

"It's over," muttered Celestine. "They're his. He's done it again, damn him."

Barbados knew he was in control. He knew what he was doing and how he was doing it and he wanted Celestine to know that he knew. He glanced in her direction, and Celestine seized the initiative by summoning her powers to blast a menacing glare back at Barbados. She cut her eyes at him, cut him deep, causing a dynamic shift in his resolve. It ruined his flow, and stole his rhythm, took the mo out of his mo-jo, and forced him to take this moment of worship in for an awkward landing.

Barbados looked over to where the small man in the rumpled black suit had been sitting, but he was gone. Barbados stood silently for several seconds, and then recited the announcement about the women's retreat from memory, managing to utter words like *bandwidth* and *neo-modern* and *sanctified unanimity*. He looked for the little man again and found that he had reappeared – this time with a look of disgust or disappointment on his wrinkled face. Barbados looked back out into the congregation and then back at where the little man had been sitting, but he was gone.

Barbados ended the announcement with a tepid reminder that the retreat would be hosted by the Sisters Working for Outstanding Opulence and Prosperity" (SWOOP), featuring a keynote address from life coach extraordinaire, Sister Celestine Nash. The theme would be "Making a Way Out of No Way: Mount up Sisters!"

4

The Headless Doll

The old woman lay flat in her neatly made bed. Her head, centered on a pillow, looked shrunken and petrified. Her eyes were set deep in their sockets, glistening with moisture, staring upward as if studying the stained and molding ceiling, evidence of a life coasting toward oblivion.

"How long has she been like this?" whispered the slender man wearing a blue seersucker suit, white shirt, royal blue bowtie, and a small lilac in his lapel providing a pop of color.

The hospice nurse stood dutifully at the foot of the bed, affecting the demeanor of a medical professional, fussing about in her tie-dyed surgical scrubs, her long elaborately decorated fingernails on display as she smoothed bed linens, and poured warm water into a smeared glass. "She been like this since I started working here, and this is my second year," she whispered.

"My Lord," responded the man. "Does she ever speak?"

"Not in the way most people know speaking," responded the nurse. "She blinks sometimes. Or she might look at you really mean if you do something that causes her pain. But the most she might do is hum one of the old hymns."

"She enjoys hymns?" asked the man as he wrote in a small leather notebook.

"I can't tell you what she likes," said the nurse, "but she sometimes hums a little something."

The man stopped writing and slid his knockoff Montblanc into his inside breast pocket. He then sat down on the bedside chair and asked, "Mother, can I share a word of prayer with you?"

The question was rhetorical. He was conversing with a woman who had not spoken in years, but it was part of the protocol to treat even the semi-comatose with respect. He smiled lovingly at the old woman's mute expressionless face. He touched her hand and began his prayer, "Lord, we thank you for the life and work of this your servant. She has toiled in your vineyard for a long time Lord, and we just ask that you be with her now as she confronts…"

Confronts what, he thought. What is causing this woman to lay here in a stupor? Is she sick, depressed, fearful, longing, diseased, or just old and worn out? What does she need from you, Lord?

ERIC D. JOHNSON

The old woman was not helping. She seemed determined to let the unfinished prayer hang limp in the small room that smelled like urine mixed with just a touch of disinfectant. The prayer meant nothing to the woman, it gave her no comfort, relieved no burden, but it did shine a big blue spotlight on the elephant in the room who had been troubling Crawford since he took the job at the CST: Did the prayer mean anything to God? He wondered if God cared about an old woman who lacked the strength to praise Him. Can God hear the silent yearnings of a soul which, over the ravages of time, has lost its soulfulness? The young man wasn't sure. He had doubts, and doubts are unsettling when your main function in life was to relieve the doubts of others.

Crawford allowed the old elephant to lumber off and take up residence in someone else's psyche. He saw the old woman's daughter standing at the door waiting for him to finish his prayer. He closed his eyes tighter and mumbled something that sounded prayerful. He hated mindless religious phrases. How many times can you "plunge your sword into the sands of time", or "lay down hymn books and Bibles to study war no more"? Do such words mean anything to a people who neither live nor die by the sword nor told time by the passage of sand through an hourglass? But these words still resonated, still held the power of transformation and comfort because prayer was communication and communication was cultural. Crawford had come to believe that Prayer was a symbol of what people expected prayer to be. It didn't have to mean anything, it did not need to have spiritual significance, a prayer just had to be lyrical, and spoken with passion.

Crawford looked at the old woman lying there with her mouth open as if she were about to speak. She's on to me, he thought. She knows I'm perpetrating a fraud. She can sense my lack of faith.

He rose to leave, pausing to look lovingly at the mummified woman, making a pastoral gesture of tapping the edge of her bed. He looked sympathetically at the daughter and the aide who each nodded at him, unknowing accomplices to a religious farce.

***

As the minister of Pastoral Care for The CST Theotis Crawford enjoyed a valued role in full-time Christian ministry. Aside from his salary and benefits, he was given a laptop, an iPhone, and a church-owned car. He knew that these perks were a 24 by 7 chain connecting him to his boss Huggey Bearman, but if working for a megalomaniac was the price for having a job in ministry, who was he to complain? "Ministry" was a bit of a stretch. His real job was to pitch the Legacy of Hope insurance program to the elderly.

Crawford accompanied the old woman's daughter to the small living room and said, "She looks well."

"She looks like death on a soda cracker," replied the daughter, a middle-aged woman named Mrs. Robinson, who wore a pink sweater that displayed two simpleton rag dolls smiling at a glittering heart.

"She seems at peace," said Crawford.

Mrs. Robinson took a long drag on her cigarette before releasing a blast of smoke out of the corner of her mouth toward a smoke filter that blew stale air from the corner of the room. "She ain't dead yet. She ain't particularly alive, but she ain't dead."

"No, praise God, she is still with us," said Crawford. It was difficult to look at the old woman and not think of her as a corpse, and if you were not careful you could make the mistake of referring to her in the past tense.

Crawford felt that the best path forward was to change the subject. "Have you had a chance to review the brochure that we mailed to you?"

The opening salvo of his sales pitch was interrupted by a man reeking of cigarette smoke, stale sweat, and fried onions who slammed into the room with the delicate grace of a drunk boarding a moving subway car. He glared at Crawford and fell clumsily into a recliner.

The woman took another drag on her cigarette before snuffing it out. She did not bother to introduce the man.

"What brochure?" she asked with a look of confusion which was valid since Crawford had never sent her a brochure.

"The brochure about the church's Legacy of Hope program."

There was a brief silence followed by mumbled profanity coming from the man in the recliner. He was covered with unintelligible tattoos that crawled up his massive arms to his neck. He sported two teardrop tattoos just under his left eye and was missing his front teeth.

"The program creates a lifetime legacy benefit in your loved one's name that will go on in perpetuity."

"In what?" asked the man, grinning like a deformed Jack-o-Lantern.

"This benefit will go on forever, in your loved one's name."

"So y'all did figure out a way to get money out of the dead. Damn, y'all good," laughed the man while spitting something out of his mouth.

"Don't be disrespectful," said the woman. "No, Reverend. We have not seen the brochure."

"And Grand Momma ain't got a dime to her name," added the man. "Y'all already got whatever money that old woman ever had, and Momma and I are broke as Hell too."

"Hush, boy. I told you not to be disrespectful. You know Mother doesn't play that."

"That's OK, Mrs. Robinson. I understand. We'll be praying for you. But please do your family a favor and take a minute to read the brochure. It describes a program that I'm sure your mother would want to be a part of. And there are some tremendous benefits for the family, especially the funeral and burial expense abatement rider."

Crawford said this while opening a fresh brochure to the section describing the funeral and burial abatement rider. It showed an attractive and neatly groomed man and woman looking lovingly into a casket.

The man stood up, swaying under the effects of booze and indignation, and said, "Do the family a favor? Is that what you just said? After what that old woman did for that church, done for the people, you got the nerve to sit here in that punk-ass suit, and talk about doing us a favor. You ought to pay for her funeral and burial, and the damn repass."

"Yes," replied Crawford, his hands trembling slightly from the unexpected attack, "We'd love to take care of all of our senior saints in the manner that you have described, but that just isn't practical."

"Prock-tee-call," said the man in a mocking imitation of Crawford's half-past twelve New England accent, which he had affected during his two years at Harvard Divinity School.

"My grandma should have been more prock-tee-call when she was giving most of her money to the church and spending what was left taking care of every baby's momma in the hood. Then y'all gypped her out of her own house. Now we got to stand here listening to you talk about doing us a favor. Man, you need to do *us* a favor and leave."

The man nodded toward the door while his mother shook her head and stared into her lap.

Crawford had barely enough time to grab his wide-brimmed cream-colored fedora and his fashionably slender briefcase as the man grabbed him by the elbow and pulled him toward the door. Crawford mumbled a stiff "Goodbye and God bless."

"Let me walk with you Rev.," said the man, whose left arm felt like a heavy length of chain as it fell across Crawford's shoulders.

"That really isn't necessary," began Crawford.

"Shut up, fool," whispered the man as he increased the force of his grip to the point where Crawford found it difficult to breathe.

"I just want to get you out of Mother's house, so I can say what I need to say."

Crawford felt like a weak child, in the embrace of a grown man.

"I need you to listen to me well," began the man. "The only favor that we need is for you to stay from around here. If I hear that your trickster con man ass has come around trying to hustle us, I'm going to mess you up. Don't think I won't. Do you dig what I'm saying to you Rev.?"

The man released his grip and began smoothing out Crawford's suit, an unexpected act of kindness.

As Crawford stood there grinning, James Brown's "*Papa Don't Take No Mess*" blared from his smartphone. Crawford quickly removed the phone from his jacket pocket and saw the digital photograph of - Huggey Bearman - leering at him.

The man snatched the phone from Crawford, laughed, and said, "Aww snap. Here is gonna be good," he swiped Bearman's digital image and answered the call.

"What's up mothel flocker? Yo, dig dis here; dis little inthurance hustle you got me runnin is tired. You got me out here husthling like a broke down hoe. Conning poor old women out their money. Find you another fool to husthle your mess. Ya, feel me pimp?" The man could barely contain his mirth. He bent at the waist and pounded Crawford's shoulder like two buddies in on the same prank.

Crawford stood with an imbecilic grin on his face as the man lisped a few more vulgarities, ended the call and tossed the phone over the fence into his neighbor's yard.

"If you want to get your phone back, I'd ring the doorbell first. They keep a crazy-ass pit bull German Shepard mix in there and the yard is full of dog crap."

The man re-entered his house, allowing the door to slam shut.

***

The smartphone, like the car, belonged to the CST, and Bearman had warned him not to lose or damage CST property or he would be castrated publicly and then fired, after paying all replacement costs. Crawford weighed his fear of public castration against the risk of fighting off the mutant dog that allegedly lurked in the yard. He was probably going to be sacked anyway, so why risk becoming dog food. It would make more sense to let the phone sit there atop piles of dog dung. Then the thought occurred to him that the homeowner could retrieve the phone for him.

Crawford rang the doorbell and was greeted with, "I already got the Watchtower," by the neighbor who spoke from behind a thoroughly closed door.

"I'm not here for the Jehovah's Witnesses," said Crawford.

"You got a warrant?"

"Why would I have a warrant?" asked Crawford, "My phone is in your yard, and I…"

"I ain't letting you in my yard or no place else unless you got a warrant?"

"You don't understand, I'm not a policeman, I just need to get my phone out of your yard. Someone threw…"

Before Crawford could complete his sentence the man behind the door muttered, "Who?"

"Your neighbor. He threw my phone into your yard. He said you had a dog in there. I just want to get my phone back."

"My neighbor? That fool crazy. Why he throw your phone in my yard?"

"I honestly do not know. But I need to get it. It's not really mine. It belongs to the church."

"The church? What church? Who your Pastor?"

"The CST, and we really don't have a Pastor, we…"

"Don't have no Pastor? What kind of church … You a storefront?"

The neighbor let Crawford enter his foyer and explained, in hideous detail, how his church was Pastored by a crooked, womanizing eighty-year-old. The house was a hoarder's delight. Crawford could feel his skin crawling as he listened to stories about how the man's Pastor was caught naked in the restroom with the 400-pound church cleaning lady. The floor was wet and spongy, and he could see tiny specs and large shadows moving in the dimly lit cave. Finally, the man led him past steaming towers of rotting food, boxes of disfigured appliances, and one shoebox that apparently held the remains of a dead cat because it was carefully labeled "DEAD CAT." The man said, "Careful, watch your step. I don't need you in here breaking up my stuff," as they advanced him through the house to the back yard.

The yard was a post-apocalyptic death-scape rivaling the set of every science fiction film Crawford had ever watched. It was filled with petrified dung heaps and smoldering piles of garbage. The garden of crap made it difficult for him to focus. Using the neighbor's telephone, (which was covered in a brownish slime) he dialed his cell phone number and located his phone, glowing and vibrating, between a salivating canine and a mangled decapitated doll.

"He might let you get the phone," said the neighbor, "but don't go near that doll. Touch that doll and I can't help you."

The phone and the doll were directly in front of the beast who had a head the size of a trash can lid. There was something off about the animal. Upon inspection, Crawford realized that the dog was cock-eyed. Its right eye peered wildly to the left, while its left eye was fixed on the heavens. The dog had one side of its muzzle curled in a jagged sneer.

Crawford edged toward the phone, trying to stay out of the dog's line of sight, wherever that was, while stepping nimbly around piles of dog dung and gnawed water bottles. As he got closer to the phone the dog rose to his feet and growled, bearing huge yellow canines.

"Can you restrain your dog?" asked Crawford.

"It's the dog's yard," replied the neighbor, "and he's territorial."

The geometry was all wrong. To avoid a rather fresh pile of feces Crawford had to take a path directly toward the headless doll, and the dog wasn't having it. He growled a low warning and moved forward, his giant head low to the ground, one watery eye fixed on a point that may have been the house or the doll, the other eye looking toward the heavens.

The dog's tail was straight down. Crawford had read that this was a sign that a dog was about to lunge. He could almost feel the wolf-headed beast sink its fangs deep into his jugular. He wondered how long it would be before anyone found his gnarled remains.

His phone played a blast of horns – indicating that a text message had been received. The horns startled the dog causing it to leap away from Crawford's path. Crawford swept in, snatched his phone, and darted through piles of dung and garbage toward the back porch.

"Nice grab!" laughed the neighbor. "I was betting on the dog to bite your ass off."

Crawford's relief reverted to anxiety when he read a text message from Bearman that stated simply "Get back now."

5

Our Lady of Domestic Violence

Crawford was relieved to see cars streaming out of the lot as he navigated his car into a parking space. This meant that his firing would not be a public spectacle but a private emasculation.

Crawford dutifully smiled and nodded at departing parishioners when he was approached by a woman whose skirt, blouse, and jacket displayed various shades of orange. The look was enhanced by her perfume which carried the scent of the Arizona desert after a hard rain when everything blooms and explodes in a citrusy orgasm. Her jewelry reflected glints of sunlight – giving her an aura of shimmering gold.

"Reverend Crawford!" gushed the orange-clad woman as she stepped into his path while extending a manicured hand. "It is so nice to finally see you here at church. When is that Pastor of ours going to let you preach again?"

"Sister! You are a sight for sore eyes." Crawford said while clasping her soft fleshy hand in both of his.

"I'm going to tell Pastor to let you back up in that pulpit. We need to see our young, handsome men up there preaching the Word."

Crawford faked a laugh and said, "Watch out Sister! I'm just a humble servant of the Lord."

The woman's gaze was half-hidden by hat shadow, giving her the look of a musketeer.

She eyed him coyly, and whispered, "Yes, we need to hear from our young men." She put undue emphasis on the word young, dragging it out so that it sounded like a growl.

Crawford stood there with her hand in his and said, "Yes, well, I've got to…" He stopped mid-sentence, distracted by another woman walking – America's Top Model style -- in their direction.

It was Janice McRae - blond hair flowing, earrings flashing, and designer sunglasses firing gamma rays in his direction.

Janice's shoes were cobalt blue objects d'art, rising toward muscular calves that tensed and released with each stride. Crawford glanced quickly at the feet of the Woman in Orange. Her shoes were impressive, but in a battle of footwear, they were no match for what was headed in their direction.

Janice nodded at the Woman in Orange and said to Crawford "Umm, if you can disengage yourself, the rest of the staff are waiting in the conference room."

The Woman in Orange slowly slid her hand from his, while glaring at Janice. Lady Orange smiled at Crawford and walked away exhibiting a catwalk strut of her own, which was curvaceously seductive and worthy of appreciation.

Janice watched Crawford as he watched the Woman in Orange and muttered something that sounded vaguely like "Fool."

***

Huggey Bearman lurked in the small reception area just outside of the conference room where the staff was assembled. He hoped that the hastily-convened meeting would create an atmosphere of suspicion, and dread.

His father, the late Reverend Bearman had beneficently ruled the pulpit of St. Stephens's for 35 years. Pastor Bearman was a man of uncommon kindness and dignity, traits that Huggey found unseemly in a grown man.

Huggey liked to think of himself as a Mack Daddy, a player's player, a rake. In his mind every woman wanted him, and every man wanted to be him. In practice, he was the type of man who would lurk outside a conference room while his colleagues were inside suffering paranoid delusions. It was the corporate equivalent of pulling the wings off flies – which he had done as a child.

"Let them sit there and sweat for a while," he thought. He saw preachers as either semi-insane do-gooders (like his father) or self-righteous con men (like Barbados). The other people were useful idiots who couldn't get jobs in the real world, so they leeched off the church. "Yea, I'll let them stew. One thing about Pop, he really believed the dribble that he preached. Not that it got him anywhere, but at least he was real." He let the thought hang while he reminisced about his father's last day on the job.

The story was retold and embellished in every bar and barbershop in town. People would say, "Yeah man. I was there when old Pappa Bear preached his last sermon. The old man got up there, took one look at that money-grubbing son of his, and his mean ass wife, and BOOM, the Lord just took him. Raptured him right up to heaven. Wasn't anything left but his body. His assistant preachers fought over the microphone like it was made of gold. They were up there stomping all over him. I heard one of his deacons lost a tooth."

The truth while less hysterical was still dramatic. The old man fell to his knees, rolled clumsily to his side, clutched the microphone to his mouth, and let out a croaking sound.

Huggey thought, "Nice try, old dude" thinking it was part of the act, the old man showing folks that he could still let the Spirit have His way. But his father's eyes rolled back in his head, and his mouth jerked to the right as though he had been fish hooked. Nobody could act that good.

A SECOND COMING

Huggey had been sitting next to his mother as he watched his father's collapse. He remembered seeing Deacon Rush fluttering around his father's prostrate body like a deranged magpie. He remembered the chaos, the pleas for help, the panic, but chief among his memories was how Barbados oozed into the pulpit, slivered past the deacons and associate ministers and hysterical missionaries. Barbados didn't hesitate; he got right into the whole Alexander Haig "I am in charge" thing. He stood up there telling people to go into prayer for their Pastor, instructing ushers to take the First Lady -- his mother -- out of the sanctuary.

In a pulpit full of toadies and lackeys Barbados was the only man in the room able to grasp the opportunity. Huggey appreciated how Barbados played the situation like a true hustler. It was a cold-blooded heartless power grab, the kind of move Huggey would have made if he wasn't nailed to his pew with a ten-megaton migraine buzzing in his head. He remembered being herded into a back room and told to take care of his mother who was screaming "Get back out there before that boy takes over your Daddy's church." But at a time when he should have been doing something, he was stuck playing nursemaid to his mother who eventually calmed, and began to mutter, "What they gonna do for me now?"

***

Bearman's thoughts were interrupted by his director of security, Major Mosono Waago whose bald head was speckled with large beads of sweat.

"Are you ready to go in?" asked Major Mosono Waago.

Bearman opened the conference room door just enough to catch a glimpse of the fidgeting staff.

Major Mosono Waago whispered, "Wait. Do not go in."

"Why?' asked Bearman, staring intently into the room.

"I need to scan the room before we go in."

"Scan the room?"

"Exactly. Who knows what they may have brought in? Especially Barbados, he cannot be trusted."

"Shouldn't you have done that before everyone arrived?"

"Exactly. This is the problem.

Bearman glared at him until Major Mosono Waago lowered his immense head and said, "I will keep my eyes open. One cannot be too cautious."

The staff sat in the boardroom, each of them attempting to appear nonchalant, content with the pantomime of the busy corporate executive: staring at smartphones, pretending to read from typed papers, busy with their laptops. Barbados sat staring at the opposite wall, without the assistance of paper or any device.

Celestine was preoccupied with YouTube footage of the last service. Her face twitched with smirks and eye rolls as she watched images of Barbados strutting and gesticulating.

A SECOND COMING

Bearman entered the conference room with his aviator sunglasses deflecting fluorescent light, his body emitting toxic levels of cheap cologne.

Major Mosono Waago held the door for Bearman and then walked around the room, stopping as he arrived behind each member of the staff. He walked behind Crawford, stopped, and glared menacingly at the back of Crawford's neatly barbered head.

Bearman assessed the group: Deacon Rush was in the house. Barbados was sitting there pretending to be in charge. Celestine commanded one side of the table flanked by her crew, that thick luscious little Teeny, and the amazon freak Janice. Crawford sat across from them, wiping his iPhone with a napkin.

Seeing Crawford obsessively wipe his phone reminded Bearman that he had given his phone to Janice so that she could call Crawford back to the office. He liked using her for clerical things like that. As he walked to the front of the room, he stopped behind Janice just long enough for her to hand him his smartphone, which she held behind herself without bothering to look at him as he took it out of her hand.

"You're welcome," she said.

"So," Bearman began, "I called you all in here because I have news, big news. News that – if we play it right -- will make our year."

He paused for a few seconds while he removed a cigar from his breast pocket, along with a folded sheet of paper. He put the unlit cigar on the table, carefully unfolded the paper, and began to read aloud:

> To Reverend Dr. Ronald Barbados,
> Executive Pastor of The Cathedral of Secular Theology
>
> Dear Dr. Barbados:

Former President Barack Obama wishes to express his sincere respect and admiration to the officers and members of The Cathedral of Secular Theology for the work that your great church has done on behalf of your city, your great state, and The United States of America.

Mr. Obama first learned of your work during his tenure as a community organizer. Your church was instrumental in developing programs that reduce incidents of domestic violence in your area and empower victims of domestic violence to recover and lead productive lives. Your efforts have become the template for similar programs all over the country and have been an inspiration to Mr. Obama and former First Lady, Michelle Obama.

Mr. Obama desires to honor the efforts of one of your members, the Mother of your church, and one of the foremost pioneers in the war against domestic violence. Mr. Obama plans to be in your area next week, which happens to coincide with the National recognition of Domestic Violence Awareness month. As part of this recognition, and to highlight the community's role in combating this attack against the American family, he desires to visit your church to honor Mother and highlight her great work.

Please contact the Office of Barack and Michelle Obama to coordinate the visit. Mr. and Mrs. Obama extend their warmest regards and look forward to meeting Mother and other members of your church.

The Office of Barack and Michelle Obama
The Obama Foundation

Bearman placed the cigar in his mouth and lit it. He puffed gently and let the blue smoke billow around his head like clouds shrouding Olympus. Then he cleared his throat and said, "Reverend?"

***

Barbados waved off the descending smoke and said, "Can I see the memo please."

Bearman slid it across the board room table toward Barbados who was now leaning forward in his chair. He stopped the sliding page and began reading silently. He could not help but notice that the memo was addressed to *Reverend Dr. Ronald Barbados, Executive Pastor*. That was him. A formal memorandum on the President's letterhead, from his President, addressed to him – the *Reverend Dr. Ronald Barbados, Executive Pastor*. "To me," he thought. "This letter, this little piece of history, this artifact for the ages, is addressed to me."

"I cannot help but notice Huggey," coughed Barbados trying to affect the measured tones of a man who was in regular correspondence with Chief Executives, "that this letter was addressed to me. I'm wondering how it came to be placed in your jacket pocket and not on my desk."

Bearman grinned and said, "When I saw the letter come in on official Obama stationary, I figured I'd better screen it."

"Screen it?" asked Barbados.

"Yea," said Bearman. "You might have gotten drafted into the Army or something."

"First off, ex-presidents can't draft anyone into anything, so, once again, you're lying. Second, we all know you're a Trump man so why would you care if I got a letter from Obama."

"I ain't nobody's man, I'm a money man."

A SECOND COMING

"He follows the money!" shouted Mosono Waago.

"If President Donald Trump is spreading the cheddar, then I damn sure will be there to get my share."

"Gotta get a share!" shouted Mosono Waago.

And if that Kenyan Obama is dropping a dollar, then Huggey gonna pick it up."

"Gotta pick it up!" confirmed the Major.

"But this letter doesn't say anything about dollars Huggey. What are you talking about?"

"See, that's why you are a preacher. Don't you realize that to Black people – especially the kind of Black folks who come to this church – Obama is the Second Coming. He's Black Jesus in the flesh, their savior, and he's coming here. This is our chance to climb solidly into the black. This is it, baby. The rainmaker is coming here to our little branch of Zion. Here to our little rock in a weary land. Here to our oasis in the wilderness, Damn! Now I feel like preaching!"

"But you wrote an editorial that Trump was some kind of economic savior for Black people," said Barbados.

"So what," said Bearman, "You can't have too many saviors. See, that's the difference between Trump and Obama."

"Tell us the difference Boss!" shouted Mosono Waago, who was now prancing from side to side like a boxer.

"See, Trump knows that a cat like me needs to get paid. Now a slick-talking dude like Obama, he figures I ought to be satisfied cause he's making me proud that he's just as smart as the white man. But see, being as smart as a white man don't feed the bulldog."

"No sir!" cried Mosono Waago.

"Naw, Doctor. Money, that's what makes the world go round and my man Trump knows that.

"Trump! He is the man, Trump!" cried Mosono Waago.

The room grew silent.

"He's right Pastor," blurted Deacon Rush. "This is ba ba big news, this is big nu news."

"I hear you Deak, but Mr. Obama isn't coming here to give us money, and he can't save us any more than Trump can. He's coming here to honor one of our members. Regardless, it will be an important, if not historic moment for our people and we must craft a reply immediately and form a committee to prepare for the President's visit."

"Not to worry," said Celestine whose face was mutating into a Ninja warrior's mask. "If there is crafting of anything to be done, my staff and I will handle it."

"The letter was written to me, Celestine, so the reply should come from me."

"A bureaucratic formality," said Celestine. "Let me remind you that we will be celebrating our Sisters Working for Outstanding Opulence and Prosperity weekend. And let me further remind you that our movement is all about Domestic Violence. I think that we are best positioned to plan and execute the President's visit. After all, he is visiting to recognize us."

Bearman savored his cigar with thoughts of sharing a Padron 1964 Anniversary Series with Obama.

Barbados looked at the letter and held it at arm's length as though reading it. "Funny," he said looking at the front and the back of the paper "But unless I'm missing something, there doesn't seem to be any mention of SWOOP."

"He mentions Domestic Violence Ronald, which is clearly a women's issue."

"It's clearly a Family issue, Celestine, and since when did SWOOP care one iota about domestic violence. You guys are all about upward mobility, women in the workplace, women in charge, breaking glass ceilings."

"Amen!" said Deacon Rush. "That's what be leading to the violence."

Everyone turned and looked at the deacon who nodded as though he had just settled the argument.

"What in the hell did he just say?" asked Teeny.

The women began to speak at once when Bearman knocked his fist on the table to restore order.

"We're getting ahead of ourselves," said Bearman. We got one little problem here that we need to solve, and that little problem – if we can't solve it – may knock out the whole visit. The question is who in the hell is the Mother of the Church. I didn't even know we had a Mother of the Church."

The room grew quiet, and everyone looked at Rush, the only man in the room who might recall the woman and her program.

"We have not had a real Church Mother in years," said Rush. "We don't have any old sisters on the church rolls ever since Miss Celestine wrote that letter kicking all the old folks out the church."

"And since when did we have a Domestic Violence program?" asked Barbados, almost to himself.

"I don't know," said Bearman, but this Mother of Domestic Violence, ran it, and we need to find her."

6

The Search

"Crawford my man," said Bearman accompanying the word "man" using his thick fingers as air quotes. "Your job is to bird dog these old folks. Do you know this woman Obama is talking about?"

Any normal Black church would easily find The Mother of the Church because Older women tend to run in packs and gather in common watering holes like the Senior fellowship or Mother's board. The CST, which took a cynical pride in never referring to itself as a church, was anything but normal.

Soon after the Reverend Bearman's death, the church staff engaged in a battle royal that pitted Bearman's son – Huggey Bearman -- against his assistant Pastor Ronald Barbados. These men were, in turn, locked in combat with Papa Bear's ruthlessly seductive executive secretary, Celestine Nash. This created a Bermuda triangle of loathing and distrust that drove people out of St. Stephens like refugees in search of a spiritual home that was less emotionally intense. This didn't bother the three combatants because they all agreed that the church needed fewer members and more money.

Intrigued by the international rise of the megachurch, and the boom of social media, Huggey and Celestine decided to align St. Stephens with a denomination known as the Secular Cathedral Ministries of the USA Inc. The denomination made a one-time monetary investment in St. Stephens in exchange for the church agreeing to live-stream its services on the denomination's website. Huggey, acting on behalf of the church, signed a contract that contained a vague and unread set of codicils listed under "Other Considerations".

Huggey and Celestine re-wrote the church's constitution and bylaws to remove authority from the Pastor and Deacons and vest power in the Human Resources department and the Finance Committee. The Human Resources department, led by Celestine Nash, issued a series of encyclicals that announced the mission and governing principles of the newly formed Cathedral of Secular Theology (CST):

- We will henceforth and forevermore be known as the Cathedral of Secular Theology (CST). We are no longer to be called St. Stephen's African Baptist

Church because we are not really African and we're not really Baptist and the word church turns people off. Besides, consumer metrics show that the word "church" trends down in the popularity index and bottoms out when combined with the word "Baptist". The words "concert" and "show" scored exceptionally high. We considered rebranding the institution as the "Worship Concert" or "Worship Show", but this didn't resonate with our focus group which broke into violent arguments over who or what they were supposed to be worshiping.

- Please be advised that all youth programs, including but not limited to: The Busy Bees, Children's Church, the Kiddie Choir, Teens for Jesus, the Boy Scouts, and the Infant Nursery will hereby become "pay to play" programs. If you want your child to participate in these valuable offerings, please complete and return the attached application and remit the appropriate fees.

- The Senior's Ministry will hereby be called "The Church Invisible". These people are faithful givers, but they are totally resistant to change. They insist on public displays of emotion, tend to pray loud, long prayers, and continue to exhibit the unhealthy

> habit of distributing hard candy to everyone in their vicinity. Elderly members (aged 65 and older) are no longer encouraged to come to church. In fact, we insist that they refrain from attending. We'll come to them. It will be easier that way, trust us. This ministry will consist of visiting the Church Invisible to make sure that they are keeping up with their Legacy of Hope payments.

The trio of Celestine, Teeny, and Janice disassembled everything that made the church a church. The CST appeared to be thriving, packed every Sunday with young, upwardly mobile, trend-setting congregants – who enjoyed attending a Gospel Concert followed by a talk show. Unfortunately, the ministries that served the community were replaced with theater groups, book clubs, and an extremely popular series of Paint and Sip gatherings.

The dwindling membership relieved the CST of the burdensome cost of ministry, but it also relieved them of having to collect money from weekly offerings. The idea was that the online congregation would make up for the lack of live attendance. But it wasn't working. Each month it became harder for the CST to show economic growth, especially since the aforementioned "Other Considerations" required them to fork over 10 percent of their revenue to the CST's National Headquarters. Profits were flat and the community around the CST had decayed and become resentful.

As a Pastoral care minister Crawford's job was to visit the sick and the shut-in. But since the church did not technically have old, sick, widowed, or orphaned members, his job became to convince people to buy into the Legacy of Hope life insurance plan – an idea concocted by Barbados and Bearman to raise funds. There was a good chance Crawford had spoken to the Mother of the Church without knowing it.

"I'm talking to *you*," said Bearman.

"He is talking to you little man!" said Major Mosono Waago, pointing a fat finger at Crawford, who looked at the finger like it was the end of a long hot poker.

Bearman said, "I figured that since you spend all day crawling through the hood trying to peddle insurance that you must have come across some old cougar who wanted to brag about being a Church Mother."

"No," said Crawford.

"No what?" replied Bearman.

"No," Crawford repeated. "I don't recall anyone bragging about being a church mother, I mean, I've met a lot of mothers who used to belong to the old St. Stephens but."

"Answer the question tiny man," snapped the Major.

"I don't know this woman."

"You smell a little like dog dookie," said Bearman.

"He stinks," said Mosono Waago.

Barbados chuckled audibly.

"Do any of you know this Woman?" asked Bearman.

The room was silent. "How are we going to find this old woman? We don't even know if she is alive or dead."

Rush raised his hand and said, "Well, I ta-tell you this. If the pra pra President Obama says she's alive, then she's alive. The government doesn't get stuff like that wrong."

"Why do you even talk," asked Teeny.

"I got a right to talk, young lady. I got a right to talk. Don't nobody say anything when you talk?"

"That's because she makes sense when she speaks," replied Janice.

"I got something to say," sputtered Rush. "Don't you tell me I ain't got nothing to say. I was in the Air Force. I know how the government works. What have you ever done?"

Barbados knocked on the conference table to retake the floor saying, "Hold on, hold on. This is not getting us anywhere. Deak makes a good point. Obama believes that this woman is alive and attends our church. If this woman is gone, or we cannot find her, then there is no reason for the President's visit."

"What are you saying Barbados," asked Bearman.

"I'm saying that if we can't find this woman we're done. You can say goodbye to your little payday. We have to either find this woman, or we have to create her."

"Until now," said Celestine, "I never understood how deluded you truly are. It's one thing for the old man to talk nonsense. No one understands him anyway. But you, you are supposed to be a spiritual leader. But this proves why your entire profession is a myth created by men to perpetuate the silly idea that preachers have some divine right to lead. We are just people Ron – not the creator – we're just people."

"Are you done, Celestine? We have the opportunity to host the first Black President of the United States. We have to take advantage of that, no matter what you think of me."

"I hate to say this," said Bearman, "but the Preacher Man is right". We have to proceed as though we know where this woman is, then we have to either find her or make her up."

"Make her up?" asked Celestine. "Exactly how do we *make up* a whole woman?"

"It's not going to come to that Nash," said Bearman, "Because Janice and that grinning idiot over there (looking at Crawford) are going to find her. They are going to look through the old historical files, they are going to interview every man, woman, and child who has lived in this neighborhood for the past 25 years, and they are going to find Our Mother of Domestic Violence."

"What if they can't find her?" asked Celestine.

"I'll fire them," said Bearman. "No. First I'll whup their ass and then I'll fire them." He glanced at Major Mosono Waago who was grinning.

"Then I'll tell the world that I fired them for stealing from the church, which is true cause we're paying them, and they didn't produce. Then I'll make Crawford put on a dress and a wig and he'll play the Mother like that old chick Tyler Perry plays, what's her name?"

"Madea, boss," replied Mosono Waago.

"Right, he'll be our Madea wearing briefs under his house dress. You like that son? No? Then find the bitch!"

"In the meantime," continued Bearman, "Barbados can write the letter back to the President."

"I reserve the right to edit and approve the letter," hissed Celestine.

"Like I care," said Bearman."

"Teeny can draft a worship program for the President's visit, and I'll approve it," said Barbados.

"We have a program!" said Celestine. "The President's visit should be included as part of SWOOP's Domestic Violence Weekend."

"You just made that up," said Barbados.

"Again, like I care," said Bearman. "Y'all work that out. The only thing I know is, we got to find that Mother, or else I hope Crawford looks good in a grey wig and a housecoat.

7

Klaatu barada nikto

Crawford was grinning when Bearman called him a "grinning idiot", and he had good reason. He was relieved that the meeting had nothing to do with his getting fired and was thrilled to discover that he had a good chance of meeting President Obama. But the reason behind his imbecilic grin was Celestine's statement "We're just people" which reminded him of his favorite line from his favorite movie the 1951 version of *The Day the Earth Stood Still*. He watched it two or three times a week and could recite long segments of dialogue from memory, especially this bit of dialogue:

"Why doesn't the government do something that's what I want to know"

"What can they do they're only people just like us".

"People my foot. They're democrats"

When Celestine said, "We're just people" Crawford wanted to blurt out "people my foot, we're Baptists!", but he quenched the urge with a self-satisfied grin.

Crawford never knew his parents, had no siblings, no cousins, aunts, or uncles. He was raised by a pious woman who called herself his grandmother, but that was speculative.

His grandmother, who worked as the house musician for a local funeral parlor, wanted him to be either a preacher or an undertaker and set him up with an agenda that consisted of Sunday school, choir practices, and an abnormally heavy schedule of funerals. She dressed him for school in suit and tie and made him carry his books in a briefcase, making him an irresistible target for every bully in his neighborhood.

His childhood collapsed into complete dysfunction when, as a 12-year-old, he preached his trial sermon. He had to stand on his toes and lean precariously forward so that he could speak into the microphone. His sermon, written on pages ripped from the back of his spiral notebook, was a trite collection of Christian sayings mixed with moralistic quips he had picked up from the host of the 700 Club. His message was simplistic and dull, yet his Pastor, a hopelessly sentimental man, told the congregation that they were witnessing the miracle of a child speaking the Prophetic Word of God. What they were witnessing was a boy artfully mimicking the flamboyant movements and churchy clichés of televangelists.

But what really made him an oddball was his addiction to science fiction. It started when the usual televangelist talk show, which played non-stop on his grandmother's television, was preempted by *Mystery Science Fiction 3000* – a show hosted by puppets who offered satirical wisecracks during the screenings of poorly made sci-fi movies.

In addition to being the weird kid who went to church all the time, he became a weird kid who rushed home from school to watch movies like *The Tingler*, *Forbidden Planet*, *The Creature from the Black Lagoon*, and *The Beast of Hollow Mountain*. Crawford was fascinated by the handsome scientists -- normally assisted by beautiful women -- who used their brains to solve cosmic mysteries.

To his knowledge, he was the only child in the history of McNair Elementary to sport a fedora and full-length overcoat, looking like a miniature gangster or tiny encyclopedia salesman – depending on your point of view. His mind ping-ponged between Christian theology and the myths perpetuated by 1950's monster films.

Recently, perhaps due to a smoldering spiritual crisis, the two philosophies began merging in his imagination. He knew that he had spent the morning praying with an old woman. He also knew he had been attacked by her monstrous grandson who commandeered his iPhone and tossed it in a yard guarded by a man-eating canine. But when he walked into the staff conference room, sure that he was going to be canned, he instead ended up on the precipice of meeting the former President of the United States.

***

Crawford sat at a worktable waiting for Janice McRae to look up from her iPhone and acknowledge him. He had been sitting there for several minutes and the woman had not so much as batted a fake eyelash. Her concentration on the small device was paranormal.

Crawford cleared his throat for the third time. In response Janice lifted her right arm and shook it slightly causing large plastic bracelets to slide down, allowing her to adjust the strands of pink-tinted hair that were obscuring her vision. Without losing eye contact with her smartphone, she said, "So, how do you want to do this?"

Crawford was caught off guard. "Well, how would you like to start," he replied stiffly.

"I don't have time for this," said Janice using her long fingers and thumbs to probe and stroke the surface of the phone. She suddenly laughed aloud and whispered "Guurl, you little slut."

"Excuse me?" asked Crawford.

"What?" asked Janice, still staring at her smartphone.

"Pardon?" asked Crawford.

"What?" asked Janice, looking up at Crawford as though she was surprised to see him. "Oh, so what were you saying?"

"I wasn't saying anything," said Crawford. "We, at least I was trying to figure out where to start our little project."

"Well, go ahead then," said Janice, still toying with her smartphone.

"Look, Janice, not to cramp your style, but it might be easier if you could take a break from looking at your phone and kind of just concentrate on what we have to do."

Janice opened her mouth wide, in mock astonishment, and said, "Are you *telling* me to put away my phone?"

"That would be a good place for us to start, don't you think? I mean, I could use your undivided attention."

"Oh really," said Janice adjusting the huge plastic bracelets and placing the phone face-up on the table. "Wow," she said while blinking her eyes rapidly. "Wow."

Crawford said quietly, "*Klaatu barada nikto*".

Janice's eyelids continued blinking as if sending out death signals to an unseen entity. She was a mystery to him. Tall, with a Hershey bar complexion. She could easily make a living as a model or, considering her well-toned body, a professional wrestler. But she was working as a fembot wing-woman for the director of human resources at a religious institution that was not really a church.

"So, shall we get started then?" asked Crawford.

Janice looked at him and cocked an eyebrow.

"Ok, so look," said Crawford. "We've got to comb through the old church records to find a woman who worshipped here during the old St. Stephens days, and used to be what was known as the Mother of the Church, or Church Mother."

Crawford hefted a box containing dozens of composition books, the kind with the black and white specked covers that were all the rage with grammar school students in the last century. There were also numerous ledgers and legal pads filled with names.

"When exactly were the old St. Stephens days," asked Janice. "I hear people all the time whispering about the old St. Stephens. What is this old St. Stephens?"

Crawford was surprised that Janice didn't know the venerable history of St. Stephens African Baptist Church – the formal name of the church from 1801 to 2000. The church had been a beacon in the community, serving as a stop on the Underground Railroad, a site for soup kitchens, and the venue for every civil rights rally held since 1950. Politicians of every stripe were known to visit. Weddings, funerals, debutante balls, St. Stephens had played host to them all. It was impossible to believe that anyone could have lived in the community for the past 20 years without any understanding of "the old St. Stephens."

"I thought you were from this area?" asked Crawford.

"I am from this area," replied Janice, "but maybe this old church didn't make an impact on people like me."

"Ok," conceded Crawford, "But it was St. Stephens for 200 years. Changing the name of the church was a huge deal. The entire deacon board – except for two or three - quit in protest. It was big news. I'm kind of surprised you don't know this stuff."

Janice quietly stared at her smartphone and Crawford decided to let the subject drop, and said, "If President Obama was aware of this Church Mother's work back when he was involved as a community organizer in Chicago then we're looking for someone who was active in the early to mid-'90s. We should find records for 1990 through 1999."

Janice lifted a stack of composition books onto the table and looked at the cover of the first book. "January 1977 to December 1977," she recited. She opened the book and began thumbing through the musty pages. Each entry showed the date when a member joined the church, their name and age, and how they joined. The abbreviation C/E meant Christian Experience, indicating the person had transferred their membership from another church, C/B meant that the person was a candidate for baptism, R was for restoration – the person had left the church and came back, and W stood for Watchcare which meant that the person was in the area for a short period and needed a temporary church home. All of this was great, but no entries indicated what a person's church title was or what ministries they served. In short, the so-called church records were useless in determining the name of the Mother of the Church.

"These funky old books are not going to help us," said Janice.

Crawford had begun thumbing through a book from January 1990 and immediately saw the problem.

"Where would a church keep its organizational records?" thought Crawford. Churches only cared about when you came and when you left. Finding records of what people did in between could be troublesome.

"Too bad we don't have annual reports or something like that to look at," said Janice. "That's why we do an annual report every year."

"Yea, an annual report every year makes sense," said Crawford, but Janice didn't pick up on his mocking tone which was probably for the best. Crawford knew that The CST's annual report was a self-serving puff piece for the denomination. It made it look like they were doing ministry work which was true if selling insurance and running self-help seminars was considered ministry.

"I think we are going to have to beat the bushes a little bit," offered Crawford.

"Beat bushes?" asked Janice.

"We're going to have to visit older members, people who remember the old church, and who may remember this Mother."

"We have no older members at The Cathedral," said Janice with indignation. "We are aggressive and progressive. We are leaning forward, not looking back."

Nice commercial, thought Crawford, "But we have older members, they just never come to Church."

"That's because we're not a church, and they are not members" Janice blew a puff of air upward to part her long pink bangs.

"Yes," replied Crawford, "but I sell them insurance. They are on my prospects list, which is identical to our sick and shut-in list."

"That is impossible," said Janice. "None of our members get sick, or old. If they become old or sick, they are, by definition, not members."

"Yes, well," began Crawford, "whatever the case, our job is to find this Mother of the Church. The only way to do that is to find elderly people who used to belong here."

Janice glared at him, this time without blinking or making a pretense of blowing her bangs away from her eyes.

Crawford returned her glare with a slight smile

8

Catastrophe

While Crawford and Janice were energized by the forthcoming Presidential visit, Celestine was wary. Fate had just nudged her closer to her dream of becoming America's next Queen of all media, the Oprah Winfrey of the new millennium. But she sat in her office silently listening for another shoe to drop.

Celestine Nash did not believe in fate; nor did she believe in luck, miracles, karma, coincidence, or divine retribution. Celestine Nash had learned through hard experience to believe solely in Celestine Nash. She held to the doctrine that truly exceptional people made their breaks and created their success and that only the weak and lame believed in fate, or faith. Yet even Celestine could not deny the existence of an invisible hand drifting over humanity, asserting its powerful command over people who had no control over the random unforeseen circumstances which could propel them toward ecstasy and fame, or deflect their trajectory downward with startling speed and ferocity.

Religious people ascribed this phenomenon to God's Grace, while non-religious believed in something akin to dumb luck. Celestine did not believe in luck or a benevolent God. If she had any belief at all it might be summed up by the Yiddish adage "Man plans, and God laughs".

But this thing with the President made her doubt her orthodoxy. A presidential visit to a floundering church had to be the result of a divine initiative.

Celestine's life had prepared her for such a time as this. She had been chosen by a heavenly selection process where God sifted through the wheat and the chaff of mindless bimbos and brain-dead dimwits until He cast His divine eyes on Celestine, held her up to the light, and found her beauty and brilliance irresistible. Celestine felt anointed (she loved that word "anointed") chosen by God to use her gifts for whatever it was that God had in mind. If the result of this Godly maneuver propelled her to unfathomable heights of fame, then who was she to argue?

But this required caution. One could not be reckless when it came to "the anointing". Look at what happened to Joseph when his player-hating brothers tossed him in a pit rather than see him gain favor with their old man. Or one might consider David, whose brothers gave him ill-fitting equipment and bad advice when he stepped up to fight Goliath.

Celestine could identify. She earned her college degree from the Albert Einstein Institute, a school that had no buildings, no faculty, no classrooms, nothing but low tuition, and a state law that allowed students to exchange life experience for credits toward a degree. Celestine had a Doctorate in life experience, having worked retail, waitressing, bartending, and the underbelly of corporate life -- telemarketing. Einstein Institute took all of this into account and allowed Celestine to take online courses toward a degree in marketing, which she selected because it reminded her of shopping, something she excelled at.

After graduation, she found work as a sales associate with a travel company. She won the job based on her marketing degree and her innate ability to give a good interview. She made eye contact and knew how to hold a man's hand just a tick longer than appropriate while applying subtle seductive pressure. Her first boss was a minor league grifter named Neil Franco, who shook her hand, looked deeply into her eyes, and was struck with certainty that this girl could make him a boatload of money. All she had to do was sit in a tiny office and sell vacation time for a non-existent South Carolina resort.

Celestine proved adept at convincing middle-aged men to buy unimproved marshland in the South Carolina Lowcountry over the venomous objections of wives who couldn't help but notice how the attractive saleswoman kept stroking their husbands' forearms and laughing at his inappropriate jokes. Frequently a man would agree to purchase the land and then call to cancel before the cooling-off period expired. This generally happened during his ride home.

Celestine showed up for work one evening to find an abandoned office. The entire operation had disappeared, leaving behind a few tattered brochures, faded posters, and a pile of broken and useless office equipment. Celestine stood there looking like a child at the fairgrounds after the circus had left town.

She walked down the street to a Karaoke bar and decided to order a last supper of hot wings and a strawberry margarita, hoping to run into some of her colleagues from the office. It was Hip Hop night at the club, which meant that college kids took the stage pretending to be Jay-Z, Wiz Khalifa, Kanye West, or The Notorious B.I.G. As Celestine was led to her table, an East Coast versus West Coast Old School rap war was playing out, starring a group of anemic white boys doing their best to upstage an ethnically diverse group of nerds led by a black kid with an extraordinarily deep voice and perfect diction.

The Black kid was short and stocky, maybe only 5 foot 3, but he did an uncanny impersonation of Public Enemy's Chuck D. Then he spit the lyrics to Biggie's "Big Poppa".

He won the contest by unanimous consent.

Celestine did not like short men, finding them domineering and mean-spirited. But she loved winners and could not resist beckoning the rap champ to her table with a crooked finger and a raised eyebrow.

Celestine slid a business card over to the fake Biggie Smalls, who was still flush from the excitement of having won a plastic microphone trophy and a $25 gift certificate for wings and beer.

He looked at the card and said, "You've spelled Entrepreneur incorrectly." His voice resonated with a deep growl.

"No," said Celestine. "I spell it "Entrepren-her" on purpose." I'm a female businesswoman. An "Entrepren-*her*."

"Deep," he replied.

"I like what you did up there. What is your name?"

"My name is Don Juan Ruckshaw or just DJ. I don't see your name on your business card."

"I don't publicize my name like that," said Celestine, sipping from her strawberry margarita. "If I want someone to know who I am I tell them. They usually remember."

"Cunning. So, am I one of the privileged few who get to know your name? Or do I just call you Ms. Entrepren-her?"

"You have talent," said Celestine. "I visit places like this looking for talent. Before I tell you my name, may I ask why you are performing in a place like this for peanuts when you could be exploiting your skills for real money?"

"This? I just do this for fun. I mean it helps me exercise my chops, but really, I'm just here to knock back a few beers and play around on the mic."

"Play around," said Celestine, looking serious to the point of disgust. "Play around," She repeated the words slowly as if saying them for the first time.

"I'm not sure you understand the type of talent that you have. But you wouldn't. People often don't. But that is my job. I find diamonds in the rough and I cultivate them into pearls."

"Are you some kind of agent or something?" asked DJ.

"No," said Celestine. "I'm more than an agent or something. I am the woman who can plug you into dreams you didn't even know you had."

"Wow," said DJ. "Deep."

"Yes, Don Juan. So, what are your dreams?"

DJ Ruckshaw explained that he was an unemployed actor, who had recently graduated from Carnegie Mellon's School of Drama. Celestine was intrigued and soon got DJ talking about the subject all unemployed actors love to discuss - themselves. He spent most of his $25 gift certificate on beer and wings, and then shots of Hennessy, all of which kept him talking. Before he knew it, he had agreed to a business relationship with Celestine that would make both rich.

Celestine knew that in an era of social media it only took one hit to make a career. Even a flop could make you famous if your life was full of insane, reckless drama. Reality television had proved that you could achieve fame without doing anything more artistically valuable than your laundry.

She created a recording company dubbed Catastrophe Records, where she would serve as the producer, business agent, and personal assistant to a rapper known as DJ Ruckus, the sole artist in the Catastrophe stable. Ruckus was DJ's nickname as a child, but only his parents knew that. He used his training as an actor to create the persona of a short, strutting, self-obsessed man who was never seen without a large Oakland Raiders ball cap, wraparound sunglasses, baggy jeans, and a ridiculously large Pittsburgh Steelers football jersey.

Ruckus was a man of mystery. Was he from Oakland or Pittsburgh? Was he blind? Was he bald? Did he have a speech impediment? Was Ruckus his real name? The only thing certain about him was that he managed to produce a hit single titled "*Bitch Can't Keep Me Down!*" which he rapped over a funky Go-Go beat made popular by 80's Washington DC funk legend Chuck Brown.

Ruckus sounded like James Brown with a bad case of laryngitis. His appeal was enhanced because only true Ruckus fans were said to understand his lyrics, and most of them were lying. His hit made vulgar references to mommas, big mommas, baby's mammas, aunties, nagging teachers, and nosey social workers, but what made the nasty diatribe a hit was that each stanza ended with the endearing tagline "…but Bitch can't keep me down!" It resonated with his audience of semi-literate teenage boys who were constantly tormented by their mommas, big mommas, baby's mammas, aunties, nagging teachers, and nosey social workers. During concerts Ruckus would strut around the stage holding his crotch mumbling incoherently:

> *"Momma always come home late,*
> *Shorty had my baby by mistake,*
> *Can a brother get some Kool-Aid with his fries and steak?*
> *But Bitch can't keep me down!"*

Celestine watched as the audience shouted out the tag line during live performances and knew instinctively what to do. She designed a line of *"Bitch can't keep me down!"* t-shirts, hoodies, and ball caps which she sold out of the trunk of an abandoned car strategically parked outside of every Ruckus concert. It wasn't long before young men would greet each other with, "Bitch can't keep me down!"

This got to be too much for women's rights groups who accused Ruckus of being part of a misogynistic conspiracy to degrade women. This backlash had two unexpected consequences. First, it turned out that no one loves a misogynistic conspiracy more than teenage boys. Second, teenage boys – especially teenage white boys -- are the jet fuel of the Hip Hop industry. Record sales flew off Celestine's poorly rendered and inaccurate sales charts, dumping tons of cash into the coffers of Catastrophe Records. There was a third consequence, which was not entirely unexpected, the entertainment media clamored for interviews with the mysterious DJ Ruckus. This was concerning because it would force Don Juan Ruckshaw to appear as DJ Ruckus – off stage. He reminded Celestine that Ruckus was an actor, that he was a classically trained actor from Dunellen, New Jersey. He didn't exist off-stage any more than Othello, Lear, or Hamlet. Celestine countered that she had never heard of the rappers Othello, Lear, or Hamlet and asked if they had representation. Cornered by the media, Celestine arranged an exclusive interview with Vibe Magazine which made journalistic history for both its brevity and lack of content:

Vibe: "So Ruckus. It's being said that you hate women and that you and your moms have beef. Can you speak on that?"

Ruckus: "Yaw, naw boss."

Vibe: "So you and your moms are good."

Ruckus: "She-ite."

Vibe: "Your hit song, *Bitch Can't Keep Me Down*, seems to indicate that you have a child out there. If your child is a girl, do you let her listen to your music?"

Ruckus: "Yaw, naw, she-ite."

The interview continued with questions from Vibe followed by unintelligible grunts from Ruckus. Finally, the interviewer asked about Celestine Nash, who was considered the brains behind Catastrophe Records. This caused Ruckus to reply in a clear vibrato, "Bitch can't keep me down!"

Ruckus next single *She-ite* failed to gain the popularity of *Bitch Can't Keep Me Down* and Ruckus came under constant attacks from the National Organization of Women, the NAACP, the National Action Network, Black Lives Matter, and the League of Women Voters.

Unfortunately for Celestine and Catastrophe Records, there is an expiration date on contrived characters. She missed the signs of her sensitive client cracking under the stress of living in the persona of a complete fool. Ruckus showed up at the Apollo Theater dressed in the Shakespearian costume of Othello. Celestine thought he looked a bit odd, but in truth, his attire was not that much different than that of the various people who were lined up outside the theater to see the show. Celestine did not notice anything amiss until Ruckus got on stage and said, "I will wear my heart upon my sleeve for daws to peck at; I am not what I am."

Ruckshaw began to suffer fits of depression and anxiety which could only be relieved by prodigious amounts of

Hennessey and cocaine. During a concert tour through Texas, Ruckus took the stage wearing the Oakland Raiders hat, sunglasses, and a jockstrap, uttering the words, "Who would not make her husband a cuckold to make him a monarch?" while glaring at Celestine who was standing in the wings with her mouth open.

Soon after the Texas Meltdown as the show was dubbed, Ruckshaw disappeared, leaving behind a single line found in Maya Angelou's "I Know Why the Caged Bird Sings":

"There is no greater agony than bearing an untold story inside you."

Investigative reporters from The SOURCE magazine captured DJ Ruckus in Mexico having allegedly undergone a sex change operation. The untold story inside of DJ Ruckus was not that he was an artistically refined actor named Don Juan Ruckshaw, but that a woman was living inside the actor who was living inside a misogynistic imbecile. Ruckshaw eventually surfaced in the United States as a deep-voiced reality TV cast member on Real House – The Jersey Shore who went by the name of Teeny. Celestine went to work as a secretary at St. Stephens Baptist Church.

9

Chief of Staff

Janice McRae, who had appeared in the one and only DJ Ruckus video as poolside vixen number 2, asked Celestine to visit St. Stephens in the hope that it would help her recover emotionally from the demise of Catastrophe records. During the filming of the video, Janice sat for hours in a lukewarm jacuzzi while DJ Ruckus pretended to rap for the camera. Sitting on the cement bench was a killer, but it was a better gig than the one she had done where the rapper used body spray instead of deodorant and smelled like rancid poultry.

Her key takeaway was that she loved the way Celestine took control of the set, the way she controlled the male models, and addressed everyone as "darling". Her dress, her hair, her makeup – were all decidedly on point.

When she heard about the crazy drama at Catastrophe records, she wasn't surprised. She felt that DJ Ruckus was a weird little dude who read books and classy magazines like

Harpers and Atlantic Monthly during breaks. But she used the humiliating sex change episode to get in touch with Celestine in the hopes of getting to know her and maybe be on board for her next entrepreneurial adventure.

Attending church was the one thing that had sustained Janice during her unexceptional acting and modeling career. Sauntering into St. Stephens wearing a sundress and stilettos gave her an emotional boost that you couldn't get from a sermon. Men couldn't get enough of her taut physique and flowing hair of whatever color matched her outfit. Women envied her style and her shoes. It just made her feel good. She figured that Celestine, being quite the stunner herself, would benefit from this kind of spiritual pick-me-up.

***

St Stephens was then pastored by Pappa Bear Bearman Sr. who was famous for calling everyone Baby or Doll Baby. His mood ranged from friendly to joyous. Each day, no matter the weather or occasion, he wore a black three-piece suit, a clerical collar, and a small silver cross pinned to his lapel.

He governed a church of slightly less than 500 people from his small office in the church basement. He was assisted by an elderly secretary who rarely worked and an elderly deacon who never spoke.

As the church grew, Papa Bear found it difficult to tend to the care and nurture of his flock, and still find the time to write sermons and keep up with the correspondence and obligations required of a pastor. Having never worked in corporate America, he sought the advice of his son Huguenot Jr. who was a financial advisor for a large insurance company and ran a Funeral Home. His son told him that what he needed was a personal assistant, someone who would handle his correspondence while he fulfilled the role of the modern Executive Pastor.

Celestine Nash became a weekly visitor at St. Stephens. She sat in the back of the church with Janice, silently plotting her personal revival while the fat little man stood up there yelling and sweating, talking about heaven and hell and Jesus and lilies in the valley and other things that made no sense to her. She simply found comfort in Papa Bear's deep soulful voice which radiated compassion.

One morning after service, Celestine was stopped in the lobby by a large man who wore a Stetson atop a leering, cynical grin.

"I'm Hugo Bearman. Who might you be?"

Celestine could not see his eyes which were hidden behind a pair of sunglasses, but his grin reminded her of the wolf in the Little Red Riding Hood fable. He extended his hand, which she took and held a tick longer than necessary, a habit she found hard to control.

"I am Celestine Nash," she replied while holding his huge warm hand.

"Aren't you the woman who represented that rapper, what was his name, DJ Roundhouse?"

"Ruckus," replied Celestine.

"What?" asked an uncomprehending Bearman.

"His handle was DJ Ruckus."

"Yea, that's right. Didn't he do the switch hitter thing, got his junk lopped off, and became a chick?"

Celestine glared at him.

"Come on girl," laughed Bearman. "I'm just funning with you. Lighten up, with your bad self!"

Celestine smiled briefly, then said, "Bearman. Are you related to Pastor Bearman?"

"Damn right! I'm his son."

"You do not talk like the son of a preacher. You seem…"

"Like a playa, like a Mack!" Bearman interrupted.

Like a fool, thought Celestine, but she said, "Well you come on a little strong."

"Me?" asked Bearman while leaning back and holding both hands to his chest with mock incredulity. "Naw, baby doll, you got this killer all wrong. I'm just a poor church boy trying to look out for his daddy."

"Really," Celestine asked. "How so?"

"The old man is spreading himself too thin," Bearman began. He is so busy nursing these sad-ass Negroes that he doesn't have time to do any of the real preacher mess that he needs to do. These people are killing him, killing the church, killing me. He needs a Chief of Staff."

"A Chief of Staff?" asked Celestine, her interest heightened. What do you mean by ``Chief of Staff?"

"You already know," replied Bearman. "Like a personal assistant. You did the same gig for DJ Roughhouse. You make arrangements, do all the behind-the-scenes stuff."

Bearman thought he was saying that he wanted a secretary to do the grunt work while his father convinced a gullible congregation to give more money. Celestine only heard the title Chief of Staff. Every other word that came out of Bearman was lost in a fog of grand speculation.

After a series of lunch meetings and one insufferable dinner, Celestine and Bearman agreed. She would control the back-office and he would control everything else.

Although Celestine had never been a member of a church, she caught on fast, having convinced herself that church services were essentially the same as rap concerts. She knew how to handle middle-aged men who, it seemed to her, were over-represented in ranks of church leadership.

She also knew how to handle groupies, who were remarkably like the women who fervently served the Pastor and the church. Celestine was the ideal woman in the ideal job, and she reveled in it until her boss dropped dead right in the middle of his sermon.

Her reliance on hip hop culture only took her so far in her understanding of the church. Older members didn't fit the mold. These people believed in whatever the Pastor was saying. Celestine understood why teenage boys loved hip hop. The cars, jewelry, liquor, and women were right in their wheelhouse. They didn't want to follow DJ Ruckus, they wanted to be DJ Ruckus. She could handle Bearman because all he cared about was money and frequent sexual dalliances with various church women, which thank God did not include her. But Celestine could not figure out what these old church people wanted, so she devised a plan to get rid of them.

Barbados was also a problem. He was an expert in the Church game, even went to college for it. To her, he was no more than a record company executive, a slick-talking good looking A and R man. The kind of guy who wanted to get in her pants and sign her acts for peanuts. Barbados wanted to control things, and men who wanted control were impossible unless you controlled them – which meant time and commitment.

What she really hated about Barbados was his hypocrisy. The way he acted behind closed doors was totally different than the stuff he preached. He taught that it was all about your brothers and sisters, but she knew that it was really all about him. Women just ate him up. She couldn't stop it and couldn't figure out how to make him go away, and part of her didn't want him to go away.

Like a lioness, she was stalking prey in the cool shadows of the watering hole. Years of fighting off tired old lions, who did nothing all day but lick their loins and salivate at the prospect of devouring her kills were finally going to pay off. All she wanted was a syndicated television platform from which she would share her vision, much like Oprah Winfrey or Wendy Williams or Rachel Ray. What better way to launch her reign as the next Queen of Media than snapping up a tasty endorsement from African American Queen, former First Lady Michelle Obama.

Mrs. Obama would be her first guest, and she would use B-roll footage as fodder for a glorious, televised ad campaign. She could see Michelle, with Malia and Sasha by her side saying, "We start every day watching Celestine Nash and her Praying Girlfriends from SWOOP!"

All she had to do was keep Barbados and Huggey from elbowing her out. Had Celestine believed in dreams or cared about truth, it was a dream come true.

10

The Silent Deacon

Mosono Waago was perched on the catwalk that overlooked the sanctuary. He crouched like a bloated jungle cat lurking behind large spotlights, peering down on the empty auditorium waiting to pounce on unsuspecting prey while they languished beside still spiritual waters. You never knew when you could catch an unsuspecting member praying aloud, bearing her soul in what she thought was a private audience with God.

Once, after a lunch of oxtails washed down with one too many Red Stripes, he decided to play God and provide answers from on high. There was a woman down below, praying loudly at the altar, asking God to send her a man to help her raise her children. She prayed on her knees with her head down making her appear to Mosono Waago like an elephant leaning in for a drink – an elephant wearing a lavender pantsuit. Stifling a chuckle, he yelled, "You are a fat lady, and your children are a fat lady's children – spoiled and greedy. No man will have you unless they like fat ladies with greedy children. Who is that man? Where is that man? Ha! He does not exist. Ha! You ask God for a man who does not exist. You are a foolish fat lady who will be waiting a long time!"

The woman shot up, looked up toward the balcony, but not far enough to see the Major who was smiling down behind the shadow of the huge lamp. The woman's mouth hung open, her eyes wide from surprise and moist with embarrassment. She was accustomed to hearing bad news delivered poorly and should have been impervious to a fool playing God but standing there as she was, in the one place where she should have expected solace, she received only the Major's hyena-like laughter.

The Major was enjoying the woman's humiliation until a man in a rumpled black suit appeared at her side. He put his hand on her elbow as if ushering her away, and while providing a kindly escort he glared up, not at the balcony, nor the sound booth, or the camera stand. No, he was looking directly into the rafters at the catwalk where Major Mosono Waago was perched. Major muttered, "What's this!" He attempted to direct the spotlight onto the man and the fat purple clad lady but instead haphazardly turned the light so that it beamed directly into his face, blinding him. By the time he redirected the spot and regained his sight, the couple was gone.

He had spied the strange, silent troll before. Usually kneeling at the foot of the altar, in deep wordless conversation. He was a goblin, more spirit than man, whose sole purpose in life was to evade The Major.

"He is in the sanctuary," Mosono Waago rasped into his 2-way radio.

"Who?" replied Bearman.

"The little man who never speaks. The man who wears a black suit but never speaks."

"The Silent Deacon," replied Bearman. "What the hell is he doing out there?"

"Nothing," replied Mosono Waago.

"He must be doing something."

"He was with a woman."

"Who?"

"A fat woman in a purple suit, a foolish woman looking for a man."

"What the hell are you talking about?"

"I do not like this man. He is quiet; he thinks he can intimidate me."

"Stay on it," said Bearman.

***

Barbados and Celestine sat in the cry room, protected by sound-proofed walls and thick windows that looked out into the sanctuary. The cry room was a relic from a time when parents brought their children to church and needed a space where they could manage the uncontrollable yelps and squeals of restless children without disrupting the service. Having corrupted the Biblical admonition to suffer not the little children, the CST prohibited anyone under the age of 13 from attending service. The room was now used for what Bearman described as VIP seating for politicians or entertainers and professional athletes who wanted to attend a church service without the drama of having to meet people.

Barbados and Celestine used the room as a demilitarized zone where they could be seen but not heard.

"What is he doing down there," said Celestine observing the Silent Deacon who was now lying face down on the floor.

While barely looking up from his notepad, Barbados smirked while replying, "He's lying before the altar."

"There was a woman with him, but she left. I bet the old pervert accosted her. Who is he talking to?"

"Seriously?" replied Barbados."

"You're going to have to do something about him," said Celestine. "We can't have him creeping around the building, popping up all over the place. It's one thing for him to come in here acting like he's praying, but now he's attacking women."

"That's Major Mosono Waago's problem," replied Barbados.

"Major Mosono Waago is a fool," huffed Celestine.

"Careful," said Barbados. "He's probably listening."

"Good," said Celestine now speaking up toward the sprinkler head protruding from the ceiling, "Now hear this, you useless turd, get that old fool out of the sanctuary."

"You're wasting your time. He only takes orders from Huggey," said Barbados. "Besides, I like having the old man around. At least he knows what the altar is used for.

"It isn't an altar," said Celestine, "It's a stage."

***

Barbados had completed his reply to the Obama Foundation. It was a well-written response that reflected the church's joy at receiving a visit from the President and their spiritual pride that he was going to be there to honor one of their own. But looking at Celestine made the entire premise of the memo feel hollow.

Something about her made him drift toward madness, a paper boat floating on a murky pond filled with uprooted trees and marsh grasses. Something about her charged his internal circuitry with the same passion that he felt when he was about to preach. She was his muse, and that he thought, was a cruel joke.

He looked down at his tablet and pressed the send key. His reply was now in the hands of the Obama team and perhaps he could escape this purgatory and this woman.

11

Secret Servant

Agent Dale Harris arrived five minutes early for his 10 AM meeting at the Cathedral of Secular Theology. To keep things relaxed and informal, he dressed business casual: grey slacks, a white button-down shirt, and a blue blazer. He was only there to find the entrance and exits, and to brief any citizens who might encounter Mr. Obama. He figured that the meeting should take fifteen minutes.

He had also arranged to meet the local police superintendent so that he could go over routes to and from the airport and local hospitals. As he approached the building, he was met by a guy claiming to be the police superintendent, but who looked like an overweight beat cop sweating profusely in an ill-fitting dress blue uniform normally reserved for police funerals, and academy graduations.

He entered the building with the superintendent and asked the large brooding man at the door for Major

Mosono Waago, Director of The CST's Safety and Security division.

"Aww, the Secret Servant," said the man as he grasped Agent Harris's hand in both of his. "Allow me to introduce myself. I am the Major Mosono Waago, retired officer in the military police, ex-New York City Detective, forensic scientist, ex-FBI agent, and a past member of Mossad."

"Honored to meet you sir and thank you for your service," replied Harris.

A group formed in the lobby which included the superintendent, Barbados, Celestine, and Bearman. They stood waiting for the Major to continue introductions, but he was basking in the phrase "thank you for your service", grinning broadly while holding the agent's hand, which he was swinging back and forth like a smitten schoolboy.

Bearman loudly cleared his throat as he pulled the Major's hand away from the agent's. "Welcome to the CST. I'm Hugo Bearman, CFO."

Major Mosono Waago was careful not to look the agent directly in the eye but instead stared past the man as though someone was standing behind him.

The agent glanced over his shoulder, shrugged, and looked past Mosono Waago as though someone was approaching the Major from the rear. The Major took a quick look over his shoulder.

Barbados interrupted the bizarre pantomime saying, "Rev. Ron Barbados, Senior Pastor. Welcome to the CST."

Celestine took the agent's hand, and while holding it gently said, "Celestine Nash, Director."

"She's the Director of Human Resources," said Barbados.

"And you're actually just the facilitator," countered Celestine who was smiling at the agent while applying slight pressure to his hand.

***

Major Mosono Waago looked over both of his shoulders, bowed slightly toward Harris, and said, "Did I mention that I once worked for Mossad."

"Interesting," said Harris. "So, you are from Israel then."

"Yes," replied Major Mosono Waago, "But I am not really from Israel if you understand."

Harris shrugged and said, "I feel like I have heard your name before. What I mean is, I have heard the words Mosono Waago, I just can't quite remember where. Where are you from?"

"Cleveland," said Major Mosono Waago.

"You don't sound like an Ohioan. Where were you born? If you don't mind me asking."

"I am asking the questions", bristled Major Mosono Waago. What is *your* name?"

Harris decided to play along, "Yes, of course. I am agent Dale Harris, but please, call me Dale."

"Ah, Dale Harris, Agent Dale Harris. Where are *you* from Agent Harris, sir?"

"Actually, I am from Ohio, Shaker Heights."

" Ah-ah!" exclaimed Major Mosono Waago. "Then this explains how you know me."

"But I don't know you," replied Agent Harris, I just think I've heard the words Mosono Waago before".

"Well, we agree to disagree," said Major Mosono Waago. "Who is this?" he asked pointing at the police superintendent.

"You know me, Major," stammered the superintendent. "We've met many times."

"You look like a man I may have met, but I do not know this fat man wearing a small, small suit. How is that suit feeling? Is that suit feeling good? That tiny suit you are wearing?"

The superintendent's face reddened as he tugged at the top of his tunic like a man seeking relief from strangulation.

"Yes, yes, I know you. But why are you wearing that ridiculous uniform? Did someone die?" Major Mosono Waago filled the room with inappropriate laughter "Yes, yes, one of your policemen has become late, and you are here to honor the life of your late policeman."

"That's enough," said Barbados. "The superintendent is here in an official capacity, so he is just trying to look official."

The superintendent nodded gratefully.

"Well," said Bearman, "Now that we're all acquainted let's get down to business. What do you need from us, Agent Harris?"

"Not much at all," said Harris. "The Supe here has mapped out the quickest routes to the hospital and the helipad so we're good there. If the good Major here can show me the entrances and exits to the sanctuary, that would be awesome."

Major Mosono Waago said, "I am prepared to show you the entire church, every nook, and cranny. The catwalks, the crawl spaces, the closets, the secret passageways. No one will elude your grasp."

"There is no need for all of that," replied Agent Harris. "The President is only scheduled for a brief visit."

"Really?" asked Barbados. "How brief?"

"I don't know," said the Agent. "Let's see," he began while flipping open his Tablet. "He plans to make brief remarks to your congregation, meet the Church Mother, present her with the Obama Community Servant Award, and then, a quick photo, then we're headed to the airport, wheels up for Brussels by 1500. We should be in and out in less than 15 or 20 minutes.

"So, when will Michelle and the girls arrive?" asked Celestine.

Harris looked confused and then reopened his device. "I show the ex FLOTUS and the kids safe and sound back at home. The children have school, and the First Lady has a meet and greet with the National Association of Organic Nutritionists. We used to call these things "Meet and Eat" but when we host groups like the Organic Nutritionists well, they are not exactly known for their chow unless you have a taste for tofu."

Celestine groaned.

Barbados said, "She's vegan."

"Oh," said the agent. "I didn't mean to offend you, it's just that…"

"You've got to be mistaken," cried Celestine. "I have it under strict confidence that the President **and** First Lady would be attending our conference on domestic violence."

"There must be some sort of misunderstanding," said the agent. "I hope the Obama Staff has not made promises that the former POTUS can't keep."

"I am sure this can be clarified," said Celestine. "Why is he even coming if he's not going to meet the women who are most affected by domestic violence."

The room descended into an awkward silence until agent Harris – his face morphing from mock concern to sheepish resignation – said, "Well, that's way over my pay grade. I'm just here to figure out how we get Mr. Obama in and out safely. So, if the Major here can show me the exits I'll get out of your hair. You might want to contact Mrs. Obama's Chief of Staff. Things change all the time. I'm really the last one to know."

"You know," said the Superintendent, the Major here is not really a Major. Major is, correct me if I'm wrong, your first name, isn't it Major?

"Really?" asked Harris. "So, your folks named you *Major* Mosono Waago. Wait!" he snapped his fingers and continued. Where did you say you were born?" "I only ask because I worked in Botswana for the Peace Corps and Mosono Waago has, let us say, an interesting meaning in Motswana.

"I told you, I am from Cleveland in Ohio. Not that it is any of your business where I am from. It is my business to know where *you* are from?"

Agent Harris held up his hands in surrender.

Major Mosono Waago clapped his hands and said, "Let us go then. I have much to show you.

"Well, I just need to see the sanctuary and the exits."

As they were leaving, Agent Harris stopped and said, "Oh, I almost forgot, I'll need the contact information for the Mother of the Church. We'll need to brief her before the visit."

"You need what?" asked Bearman.

"The address and phone number for your church Mother; the woman that the President is coming to visit. It's just routine. We always conduct an informal briefing to make things go smoothly on the day of the visit."

Barbados exchanged a conspiratorial glance with Bearman.

"If you could just look that up for me, I'll pick it up before I leave."

With that, he strode out of the area with Major Mosono Waago and the Superintendent in pursuit.

"Whose address are we going to give this agent?" asked Barbados.

12

The Mothers Address

Major Mosono Waago led Harris and the Superintendent up the narrow metal stairway toward the catwalk which overlooked the sanctuary. The stairs sagged and swayed under the weight of the three men, and Mosono Waago looked back frequently, delighted by the effect that the trip was having on the superintendent whose face was red and sweaty.

Harris followed obediently, staring up at two sets of huge rear ends, wondering why a man would voluntarily go by the name of Mosono Waago – which in the Motswana language could be loosely translated to mean "ass hole". Botswana was a lovely country, rich in gold, diamonds, beef and apparently biting desert humor. "Major Asshole," Harris thought. He had once worked for a Major Woody, but at least that was the man's real name and came with a certain sense of sophomoric panache. Harris's attempts to suppress his laughter caused him to groan audibly and try to disguise his mirthful outbursts as coughs.

Major Mosono Waago wheeled, catching him in mid-giggle, and said, "You find something amusing?"

"No, ass…No Major," his face reddened with a laugh stifling effort. He wondered if the Supe knew of the Major's unfortunate name. He'd have to save it for the post-visit briefing, over a beer.

Harris hated wasting time. He could see the catwalk from the floor of the sanctuary so there was no need to make the climb. He would of course have the area checked just before the President's arrival, but it was common knowledge that – except for that horrible day in Dallas – assassins seemed to prefer their attempts up close and personal. The President was in greater danger from an old lady with a hatpin than some dude lurking above the church with a high-powered rifle. But here he was, crawling behind the fat ass of the Major, doing recon to prevent some wannabe Manchurian Candidate from taking a pot shot at the ex-POTUS.

Major Mosono Waago stopped and said, "Look down there, at the front of the sanctuary, do you see him?"

"See who?" asked Harris.

"He is down there," rasped Mosono Waago. "You see him don't you."

Harris saw the back of what looked like a small man in a black suit, on his knees, his forehead pressed against the first step leading up to the stage.

"You mean that little man, kneeling?" asked the Superintendent.

"Exactly!" cried Mosono Waago. "That is highly irregular."

***

"Klaatu was deep," thought Crawford, while resting in the quiet embrace of a yet another daydream. "His wisdom came from a true understanding of patience, a natural understanding that man's real problem was not greed or envy but a restive need to get what they want when they want it." Crawford had explored this idea in his master's thesis richly titled: *The Virtue of Klaatunian Patience in The Day the Earth Stood Still: A Message for the Post-Modern Church*. His mentor, a Greek antiquities scholar named Lucius Katz had to view the film several times before he could effectively critique Crawford's work, and even then, was unimpressed, calling the movie a "rather obvious attempt at a metaphorical Christ." He accepted Crawford's work since it was at least not another thesis based on the Star Wars trilogy.

This did not prevent Crawford from building a paradigm with *The Day the Earth Stood Still* as its primary philosophical pillar. Crawford theorized, usually privately, that Klaatu being mankind's intellectual superior had to figure out a way to prove his power while at the same time satisfy man's need to get to the point. He could have satisfied man's reckless impatience by using an atomic bomb in the manner used by the United States during World War II, but that would have made for a crass farcical short film where Klaatu beseeches Gort to turn the Washington Monument into an anthill.

Crawford couldn't completely mine the philosophical depths of *The Day the Earth Stood Still* while he sat in the presence of Janice McRae. She was an alien life-form impervious to logic, a self-absorbed feline that lived by reflexes and instincts. A distraction.

While Crawford shuffled through box after molding box of ancient church records, Janice sat there gazing at her smartphone or carefully inspecting her impeccably manicured fingernails or toying with long locks of synthetic blue hair.

The leading men in the 1950's era science fiction classics that Crawford adored, were generally accompanied by female side-kicks who sublimated their brilliance to that of the scientist so that he could defeat whatever evil was threatening the world. Altaira (played by Ann Francis) from the 1956 motion picture *Forbidden Planet* de-sexualized her attire so that she would appeal to Commander John

Adams (played by Leslie Neilson). Would Janice hide her long muscular arms or wear flat shoes so as not to reveal the slope of her back or the round form of her backside? Would she take her sexuality down a notch for the betterment of the planet?

No Crawford conjectured. Janice was clearly a victim of the 1956 classic, *Invasion of the Body Snatchers*. She was one of the pod people, devoid of emotion and feeling, walking around in a real woman's body. Somewhere, there was her body double, a warm loving woman with a big black afro, lying in a pod, waiting to snatch the body of Janice McRae, give her a soul, some humanity.

"Why are you staring at me?" asked Janice.

"I'm not," stuttered Crawford, "I was just thinking, hoping, that you would look through some of these old notebooks. I could use the help."

Janice picked up an old composition book and began thumbing through the pages. She was about to explain to Crawford that this was a waste of time when Bearman exploded into the room.

"What are y'all up to in here? You trying to snake up on my woman, Crawford?"

"Me, snake, what?" said Crawford.

"That's how you slick college boys do it right? Snake up on the other brother's Bae. Well, I ain't the one partner. I admire your player though."

"I'm not doing whatever you think I'm doing sir," said Crawford, feeling like a man who had been caught elbow-deep in the cookie jar.

Janice looked at Crawford with one suggestive eyebrow raised.

"I ain't mad at a man for being a man," said Bearman. "I didn't know you had that dog in you, but I ain't surprised either. My daddy was a preacher. I know all preachers have a little dog in them."

Janice grunted and blew blue bangs out of her face.

"But that ain't why I'm here. I need an address for that mother of the church, and I need it now."

"Well sir," began Crawford haltingly, "We really have not had the time to fully examine all …"

Bearman cut him off with "I just need one address fool."

"But what if the address isn't the real mother?"

"Well, she sure as Hell has to be somebody's mother."

"Yes, but I think the President is looking for a specific mother."

"We ain't got time for all that," said Bearman. "The man is here now, and he wants that damned address!"

"The President is here now?" asked Crawford.

"No fool. The President's white boy is here checking out the place with Major and he wants the mother's address."

There was a moment of silence while Crawford searched his Rolodex of lies and lame excuses to find something fitting the occasion.

"Give him this," said Janice "pointing to an entry in the composition book that Crawford had just handed her. "This is the mother."

"See," said Bearman, "That's why women run the church. They make things happen. You sitting there talking about "What if this ain't the real mother."

Crawford looked down at the name and the address written in neat cursive handwriting on the blue-lined page. Both the name and address were familiar to him because – as Satan, the God of calamity and misfortune would have it – he had just visited that address and had been warned never to return.

***

Major Mosono Waago escorted Agent Harris and the Superintendent into the executive conference room where Bearman, Barbados, and Celestine sat waiting. The Superintendent's pants were covered with dust, especially his right side which was peppered with yellow and white stains.

Agent Harris had small stains on the knees of his slacks, but otherwise, he looked like a man who had just enjoyed a brisk walk through the countryside.

"Your Major here took us on quite an expedition," said Harris.

"You look like you have been rolling around in bird mess Supe," said Bearman.

The superintendent looked down at the yellowish stains streaking down his right pant leg and released a loud groan.

"That old man, the Silent Deacon. We had him under surveillance. He is very elusive, but we tracked him from the stage to the grotto in the courtyard, said Major Mosono Waago.

"Your Major here seems a tad obsessed with one of your parishioners, who, as far as I can tell does nothing but pray," said Agent Harris.

"I need to point out," said the Superintendent "that Major Mosono Waago is not really a Major, I mean he doesn't have a rank, he's…" The superintendent did not finish his thought but looked at Barbados in a vain appeal for help.

"It is highly irregular behavior," blurted Major Mosono Waago. We cannot have this man, who never speaks, wander all over the building. Just praying here and there, just praying and praying. Who is he praying to? Why does he not speak? It is highly irregular."

"I'm no expert," said Harris, "but isn't that the whole idea of a church?"

"We are not a church," said Celestine. "And today I saw that man accost a lady, right in front of the stage."

"He's harmless. He's a harmless old man that likes to pray in church. Let's not make a big deal out of this," said Barbados.

"This is not a church," said Celestine, this time with an air of exasperation as though she were talking to a room full of idiots, "And this man is dangerous".

The Major was thrilled to have an ally, "Yes, he is extremely dangerous. You do not know about these people, these people who wander around. Where does he go? Where is he from? If he talks only to God what does he say?"

The room grew silent as everyone contemplated that question. Finally, agent Harris said, "Maybe I should just get that contact information and be on my way."

13

The Bishop

The women were glowering at Barbados - silently voicing their collective discontent at his indifference to Celestine's concern that the Silent Deacon was a pervert. They then began exchanging menacing whispers, followed by dramatic eye-rolls enhanced by fake eyelashes and hostile applications of mascara. Barbados didn't seem to care, but their act worked on Crawford who felt like he had wandered onto the set of the *Big Sleep* a 1946 noir classic that had a famously convoluted plot and multiple femme Fatales. He fiddled with his pen and notepad; an honest man caught in the middle of a bizarre criminal enterprise.

Crawford was almost convinced that the entire presidential visit was part of an elaborate con game where you convince thousands of people into attending a church service where they will get to meet the first Black President of the United States. You take up a huge offering, then, when the guest of honor never shows up, and make a run for it leaving a hapless associate preacher - like Crawford - to deal with thousands of angry church people. He wouldn't last 5 minutes. They'd probably hang him upside down in the church parking lot.

He had not actually seen the Presidential letter. For all, he knew Bearman, and Barbados had written it themselves. He recalled how Huggey had quickly accepted the first address for The Mother that Janice provided. It was too convenient, too easy. Then there was the preposterous charade of Huggey allowing Mosono Waago - a known moron - to plan security for a Presidential visit with a representative of the United States government. Something was wrong.

The only positive was the possible takedown of the Mother's grandson. He had to appear prominently on somebody's rap sheet, so it would not be long before the Secret Service discovered that he was a murdering, drug dealing, troglodytic, thug. At a minimum he had warrants for unpaid child support, weapons offenses, breaking, possession with intent, the usual crimes, and misdemeanors common to men of his ilk. This was assuming that the secret serviceman was a federal agent and not an actor hired by Celestine Nash who had once threatened to hire actors to portray preachers during the morning services.

As he rummaged through possible conspiracy theories, he was comforted with the thought that any conspiracy would require cooperation and trust among the co-conspirators. The idea that Huggey, Nash, and Barbados could trust each other was laughable. He was certain that Nash didn't know the meaning of the word and that Huggey didn't even trust himself. No, a conspiracy of this sort was beyond them.

It was at this point that Bearman abruptly began the meeting.

***

"Does that blood-sucking leech know about this?"

Huggey was directing his question at Crawford and Barbados because as ordained clergy they were the only ones in the room who were granted the privilege to speak to the alleged blood-sucking leech who served as the Bishop of their denomination: The Secular Cathedrals International, not to be confused with the Secular Cathedral Ministries of the USA Incorporated.

The CST was bound by a contractual arrangement that gave 49% of all operating revenue to the Secular Cathedrals International. The agreement was negotiated a year after the death of Rev. Bearman when St. Stephen's church was saddled with debt and had no income. During this time, Barbados, Huggey, and Celestine were intertwined in a three-way civil war. Huggey hired street people to stand and shout Bible verses whenever Celestine attempted to read announcements. His favorite being (*1 Corinthians 14:34*):

Women should be silent during church meetings. ... Let your women keep silent in the churches, for they are not permitted to speak; but they are to be submissive,

Whenever Barbados stood to preach. someone would shout out: (Matthew 24:11): *Many false prophets will arise and deceive many* and then storm out.

All of this proved too much drama for some people who came to church for enlightenment or encouragement. People left the church and those who stayed were there only to witness the spectacle. The church's treasury plummeted, and the bank was close to foreclosing when the Bishop of the Secular Cathedrals International came to the rescue. He gave each of the three combatants a form of power: Barbados got to preach, Celestine got to manipulate people as Director of Human Resources, and Huggey got to handle the money. The cost of the compromise, 49%, seemed remarkably low.

***

The Secular Cathedrals International (and the Secular Cathedral Ministries of the USA Inc., and the Secular Cathedral Ministries of America Inc.) were the brainchildren of The Bishop and Entrepreneurial Apostle R. X. Sandman. Sandman labeled himself an apostle because he claimed to have had a personal encounter with God which he explained during a live radio broadcast of *Claim Your Blessing Now!*

He began the historic session by giving his testimony:

"I was performing that old Temptations cut, *Ain't Too Proud to Beg*, at the Sky Port Lounge in Pooler, Georgia. It was part of a classic R&B review that we used when there were a lot of middle-aged white folks in the room. They like that sort of thing. So, I'm up there on the bandstand and I see this cat sitting in the corner. He was wearing a blue sharkskin suit, sharp but not too sharp if you know what I'm saying. But he's not nursing a drink or anything. He's just sitting there, watching the show. I couldn't tell if he was digging the act or not, so I said to him, 'What you want to hear, partner? What can I sing for you that will make you want to buy a drink, order some food, and leave a big tip?' He looks me right dead in the eye and he says, "Sing *In the Garden*." That kind of messed with me because that was my Grandmother's favorite hymn. You know it:

> *I come to the garden alone;*
> *While the dew is still on the roses;*
> *And the voice I hear falling on my ear;*
> *The son of God discloses.*
> *And He walks with me, and He talks with me*
> *And He tells me I am His own;*
> *And the joy we share as we tarry there;*
> *None other has ever known.*

Here I am doing my Eddie Ruffin thing, got the room rocking, and this cat wants to hear some old church music? But even though it was the last thing I wanted to do, I had to sing it. Something got hold of me, you know what I mean. I knew the words, but I didn't know them, you know what I mean. But if I kept my eyes on that man in the blue suit, I could sing it as though I wrote it.

And he said to me, you are singing in this little room in Georgia, but I tell you, you are going to sing this song in front of thousands and hundreds of thousands.

Then he was gone.

I told my momma about it and she said, Boy, that was nobody but the Lord. I have been preaching His Gospel ever since.

I preached Him on buses and trains and street corners. People would just come up and hand me money, big money, not no dollars, and fives, but hundreds and thousands. And all I'm doing is telling folks what they need to do to get straight.

***

Bearman never believed a word of it. He knew Sandman had shrewdly built a religious empire by buying a controlling interest in struggling churches and converting them into his brand of prosperity Gospel enterprises. Sandman understood that churches were always looking for ways to stay solvent and he provided the way. Bearman's chief role at The CST was to generate revenue and then keep the money out of Sandman's hands. It was difficult because Sandman refused to talk to him.

"If Sandman finds out about this visit, he'll want to get his beak wet, so we need to keep him out of the picture," said Huggey.

"I have not spoken to His Grace about this, but I can't see how we are going to keep it from him," said Barbados.

Bearman paced the room, groaning and stroking his chin.

"This is becoming a nightmare," said Celestine. "No First Lady, no Sasha, and Malia, God only knows who the Mother of the Church really is, and now we can't even promote the visit?"

"Oh no'" said Huggey. "We have to promote it. How else are we supposed to sell tickets?"

"Excuse me?" asked Barbados while spinning 360 degrees in his conference room chair, an acrobatic stunt he liked to perform during meetings when someone, usually Celestine, said something he found undeniably stupid.

"What?" asked Huggey. "You think we gonna sit here and let these people just waltz up and meet the President for free. You think we're going to rely on one of my daddy's damned free will offerings. The Devil's a liar!"

Barbados turned to Crawford and asked, "Are you hearing this?"

Crawford responded, "Well our Jewish friends often have to have to pay their temple dues to secure a seat during the high holy days, so this…."

"That was a rhetorical question dummy," interrupted Barbados.

"You gonna let him talk to your man like that?" Huggey asked, directing his question at Janice.

The room grew quiet as Barbados and Celestine looked at Crawford whose brow instantly became coated with sweat. Janice, who was studying her fingernails, arched one eyebrow but that could have been a reaction to a slightly misaligned cuticle.

"I've already got Teeny working on getting the flyers and tickets printed up," continued Huggey. "Balcony seats start at one hundred bucks. The first two rows in the center pews are going for twenty-five hundred a pop. Celestine, you got to tell them ushers to stack people into them pews like Africans on a slave ship."

"Next you are going to tell me you are charging for the church bulletins," muttered Barbados.

"Twenty-five dollars apiece," growled Teeny.

"If we do this right, we can gross a half-million bucks, then a half-million more on residual sales," smiled Huggey.

"Residual sales?" asked Barbados.

"CDs, t-shirts, hats, mugs. Stuff you sell people who weren't' there so they can act like they were. Then of course my book deal."

"Your book deal?" asked Barbados who was now spinning constantly in his chair. "How can you parlay a 5-minute Presidential visit into a book deal, unless it's a matchbook."

"Story about how my daddy built this church into what it is today and how the President of the United States came to pay homage. It'll be mostly pictures, right Teeny?"

"Photographs," said Teeny.

"That ought to be worth at least another half mil, not counting TV and movie deals. Me and Teeny bout to blow up!" At this Huggey and Teeny slapped hands high-five style while Celestine eyes blazed "whose team are you on" lasers at the place where Teeny's Adam's apple should have been.

"Don't worry," continued Huggey, "there's something in it for all of you. That's why we can't let that greedy little schmuck sink his teeth into this".

"Well, sir. His Grace may already know something," said Crawford. "He responded to our monthly sales report with a note indicating that he will be attending a worship service here shortly.

14

The Briefing

As the meeting ended, Huggey said, "Hey, I just got a text from the Major. The secret service guy is going to brief the Mother tomorrow at her house. Crawford, I want you to be there."

Crawford searched in vain for a fitting excuse. The only thing that came to mind was a pathetic "Sorry boss but the Mother's monster of a grandson warned me – upon penalty of death – not to darken his doorway. So, I think I'm going to pass on the briefing."

What he actually uttered was worse: "Deacon Rush should go; I think he might know the Mother better than me and he…"

"Bullshit," said Bearman. "I can't have that stuttering fool messing up this deal. You're going."

"He's right," conceded Barbados. "We need a professional in there explaining why Mother must attend this service. Who knows how she'll react to the invitation after the way Celestine treated her and other elders of the church?"

Celestine responded, "Oh my God. People want to be surrounded by youth and beauty. I have nothing against old people, but they just don't drive the numbers. I mean, do you ever see old people – with their ridiculous hats, and their hard candy, and the constant fanning - in the studio audience of *The View*?"

"I don't know what numbers you're looking at," said Bearman. "We did pretty well with their bake sales and what did we use to call it Rev?"

"Love offerings," said Barbados.

"Damn right," said Bearman. "I loved the love offerings."

"The cakes and pies were pretty good too," said Barbados.

"The life of the church!" said Bearman while smacking hands with Barbados. "Now we're broke. That's why I had to pimp out this fool to sell life insurance," he said jabbing an unlit cigar in Crawford's direction.

Crawford felt like he was being crushed between the pincers of a giant ant, like the monsters featured in the motion picture *Them!* another of his sci-fi favorites.

Smelling fear, Bearman asked, "What's wrong boy? Oh wait, I get it, you want your woman to go with you? Fine!

Janice, go with this fool so he can show you what a man he is. Let you see how he handles his business."

There was a moment of uncomfortable silence before Janice said, "What time you gonna pick me up?"

He looked at Janice and instead of seeing the stoic face of a sister who would not be pushed around he saw a girl who wanted to know what time she was being picked up for the senior prom.

"Nine thirty," muttered Crawford, his head down.

Bearman leaped in the air like he had been shot in the backside, and cried out, "Aw, it's like that! Damn, y'all gonna plan your little date right in front of me. Barbados, your boy might have a pair after all."

***

The sky was a mix of ashen grey mist and brown haze giving the day a funereal feel, cool and deadly. Crawford was dressed in a dark blue suit to match his mood which was a combination of dread and hopelessness. He wanted to pick Janice up at her home, but she insisted on meeting him at a coffee shop in her neighborhood which was close to the Mother's residence.

He saw her sitting at an outdoor table sipping from a paper cup, staring into space. She was wearing a teal scarf that was wrapped around her neck like an anaconda. Her sunglasses – totally unnecessary on a cloudy day – had bright red frames to match her blazing red lipstick, which was offset by her hair, which today was pale yellow.

"Good morning Janice," he said.

"I bought you a coffee," she said pointing to another paper cup on the table. "You can doctor it up inside with sugar and cream."

"Thank you, Janice. I appreciate that, but I don't drink coffee."

"You're going to need it today," she responded.

Crawford thought of the giant grandson waiting to squeeze his head until it popped off his neck and figured that a jolt of caffeine might sharpen his fight or flight instincts.

He entered the shop and dumped a couple of packets of raw sugar and a healthy dose of half-and-half into his cup. It was light and sweet, an emasculated brew, but one sip went right to his head. He returned to the table finding Janice still sipping and staring.

"You ready to go?" asked Janice.

The timing was crucial. Crawford wanted to arrive right after the special agent. He had to make sure that an armed lawman was on site when they entered the house and confronted the grandson. That way the agent could step in and keep the maniac from throwing him through the picture window.

"We've got a couple of minutes," said Crawford.

"I thought you were the kind of brother who liked to get to meetings early," said Janice.

"Normally," said Crawford.

As he sat at the table, he saw in the distance what looked like a drunken bear, staggering toward them, swaying in different directions, stopping, doing a little off-balance dance, and then staggering forward again.

"Look at that fool," said Janice who had also caught sight of the bear. "Not even 9 o'clock and he's already straight up blasted."

There was something familiar about the bear's gait, the shape of his body, the way he let his massive arms dangle to the side, more primate than ursine, like a gorilla wearing a bear costume. It also seemed to be wearing army issue fatigue jacket and trousers that were sagging almost to his knees. "My God," Crawford thought. 'That's the Mother's Grandson."

"Let's get going," he said aloud, nearly knocking his cup off the table.

"Chill," said Janice.

Crawford's mind processed images of teardrop facial tattoos, a toothless grin, and of him crawling through feces while fending off a savage dog.

"No time to chill," rasped Crawford. "We need to get to Mother's house now. I don't want him to see where we park.

"Who?" asked Janice.

"Let's leave now, please."

"You coming on a little strong," said Janice, her eyes peering over designer glasses, one hand on her hip, the other holding a cup of coffee.

Crawford had planned to open the door for Janice, always a nice touch, but there was no time. Instead, he threw himself into the driver's seat, reached over to unlock and push open the door so that Janice could ease her six-foot frame into the passenger seat.

Crawford started the car and threw it into gear, barely giving Janice time to close the door.

"Oh my God," she said while squeezing the coffee cup, loosening the lid and allowing the coffee to explode out of the cup, slosh down the sides, onto her hand, and cascading onto her cream-colored skirt.

"Yo dude!"

"Sorry, Janice."

Crawford lurched his car out of the parking spot and made an illegal high-speed U-turn, crossing in front of oncoming traffic, and roaring up the street. As he passed the Mother's house, he jerked the steering wheel hard left causing the car to spin into another U-turn. Then he sped into an open parking space directly across the street from Mother's.

Janice sat, coffee dripping from her shaking hand, sunglasses askew, a teal scarf covering her nose and mouth like she was a bandit.

Crawford was nonchalant.

Another car had just parked across the street, directly in front of Mother's house. The special agent exited that vehicle and gave a military salute.

"Hello, Reverend. Ms. McRae. That was some maneuver you just executed, Reverend. Did you attend a Tactical Evasion Driving School? I'm impressed."

"Greetings special agent. No, I just, well I thought you should have the most convenient spot outside the house."

"Did you have a little accident there, Ms. McRae?"

Janice looked down at her crème colored skirt, now decorated with an elaborately designed coffee stain.

"Aww man!" she said while throwing the coffee cup onto the sidewalk. "Are you serious right now?"

The agent was looking for the Mother's house address and Crawford's focus was locked on the Grandson who was still lumbering up the street.

"Seriously?" said Janice, noticing that she was being ignored by two men too stupid to understand the ruin of a designer skirt.

"All right," said the agent. "Let's go in and brief this Mother. Maybe they have some club soda or something to deal with that stain."

Crawford rang the doorbell and the threesome waited until Mrs. Robinson, the Mother's daughter, answered the door.

"Mrs. Robinson, it's so good to see you again," said Crawford, summoning the smarmy charm of a two-bit insurance salesman.

"Come in," said Mrs. Robinson.

"Yes, thank you," said Crawford. "This is Miss Janice McRae from the church, and this gentleman is…" Crawford hesitated. He couldn't remember the agent's name. He looked at Janice who was busy studying her stained skirt. He looked at the agent who was grinning at him.

"I'm Maxine Robinson," said The Mother's daughter, extending her hand to the agent. "You must be the FBI man."

"Not even close," said the agent. "I'm Dale Harris, part of President and Mrs. Obama's secret service detail."

"It's an honor to meet you, Mr. Harris. How's the President doing?"

"In a few days you can ask him yourself," said agent Harris. "He's anxious to meet you and Mother Robinson."

"Can I offer any of you something to drink?" asked Mrs. Robinson. "I can put some coffee up or heat some water for a little tea."

"Definitely not coffee," said the agent. "Miss McRae is wearing hers, and the way Rev here is driving I wouldn't want to see what he's like with caffeine in his system."

"Me either," muttered Janice.

"Oh child, you've spilled coffee all down that cute little skirt. Do you need something to blot it with?"

"No," said Janice. "I'll get it cleaned."

Crawford had maneuvered himself so that he had a good view of the front door. He could also see a portion of the porch and front steps.

"Well, I guess you all want to see Momma. As soon as he gets here, I'll take you back," said Mrs. Robinson.

"Oh, I don't think we need to wait for him," said Crawford.

"Well, you can't talk to Mother without him," said Mrs. Robinson.

"I've spoken to her several times without him here," said Crawford through teeth locked in a fading smile.

"You may have prayed over her," said Mrs. Robinson, "But I don't think you've ever had a conversation with her. She doesn't talk to anyone unless he is right by her side."

Crawford looked at his wristwatch and said, "Well, I know Agent Harris here is busy and Janice and I have to get back, so I think we can cover what we need to without your son."

"My son?" asked Mrs. Robinson.

"I'd like to meet your son," said Harris. "Will he also be joining you at church to meet Mr. Obama?"

"Ha!" snorted Mrs. Robinson. "It will take more than a miracle to get that fool in a church. Lord knows Mother tried to keep him in church and prayed up, but it didn't do good."

"Well since he isn't going to be part of Mother's official delegation then I see no need of…"

Crawford's attempt to bum rush the proceedings was interrupted by the doorbell ringing once.

"Here he is," said Mrs. Robinson.

Instead of opening the front door, she went to the back of the house toward the kitchen. Crawford opened the front door. No one was there.

"He's going to ambush me," said Crawford.

"Who?" asked Harris.

"The son, the son, he must have recognized my car. He's planning an attack."

"Why would he ring the bell to get in his own house?" asked Janice.

"He was obviously trying to lure me to the door. When I didn't take the bait, he ran around back to use the rear entrance."

"What have you ever done to him?" asked Janice.

"Long story," replied Crawford.

Mrs. Robinson returned and said, "Y'all can go back now. They're ready."

Crawford figured he was probably safe in the Mother's tiny bedroom with two witnesses. But he thought it best not to take any chances and let Agent Harris and Janice lead the way.

***

Nothing had changed since Crawford's last visit. The room was dark and still smelled of disinfectant and urine. The Mother still lay flat in her bed, shark-like eyes staring up, breathing faint, showing negligible signs of life. But this time, half-hidden in the shadows was a small man in a rumpled black suit. The collar of his white shirt was yellowish and frayed, his black tie, worn and faded, hung limply around his neck. He wore a wonderful black fedora, the type of hat that was fashionable in the 50s and was now making a comeback. He was too small for his suit and the hat obscured his face to the point where he didn't appear like a man at all, but like a shadow dressed in semi-formal attire.

"Deacon," began Mrs. Robinson, ``these here are the folks from the church who have been wanting to speak to Mother about coming back".

He removed his hat revealing a thin layer of hair the color of cotton.

He said nothing.

"Isn't that the little guy that prays at your church?" whispered Harris.

"Impossible," said Janice. "I've never seen him and even if I had we do not have anyone of his age attending the CST."

"No," said Harris. "I'm positive he's the guy that put a scare into Major Dumbo."

"The Silent Deacon," said Crawford reverently.

"Urban legend," hissed Janice.

"Well, he is a Deacon," said Mrs. Robinson. "At least he used to be back when Mother went to old St. Stephens."

"We no longer have Deacons, and we are not a church, at least not like the old gender-aggressive St. Stephens," said Janice who had managed to twist her skirt so that the coffee stain was now running along her hip.

"Then this guy must be some kind of ghost," said Harris "because I saw him praying at your church and he spooked the hell out of Major Jumbo."

"The silent Deacon," said Crawford again. He had heard that Reverend Bearman's old deacon attended services at the CST, but he had never met him. Huggey and Deacon Rush claimed to know him but only Barbados and the Major claimed to have seen the man in the building, and neither of them was sure.

"Greetings sir," began Crawford, who was relieved not to be facing the Mother's grandson and intrigued to finally meet the legendary Silent Deacon.

Crawford reached out to shake the Silent Deacon's hand, but the old man was staring at the Mother. The old deacon placed his small, weathered hand on the Mother's forehead and closed his eyes.

"Is he praying?" asked Crawford.

"I believe so," replied Mrs. Robinson. "He always does that. Actually, that's all he does and then he just leaves."

"I love the man's brevity," said Harris.

"So, continued Harris. "Mother doesn't look too well. Will she be able to attend church on Sunday?"

The old man removed his hand from the Mother's brow, looked directly at Harris, and nodded his head one time indicating the affirmative.

"So, I can take that as a yes?" asked Harris.

"I think so," said Mrs. Harris, "that's the most I've ever heard him say."

"But he ain't said a mumbling word," said Janice.

"Should the church send a car for the family?" asked Crawford.

The old man made a subtle head movement and placed his hat on his head,

"He said no," said Mrs. Robinson.

"He didn't say a thing," said Janice.

"I know, but that's what he does when I ask him if he's staying for dinner. So, I think he means no."

"We'd get a lot more done in Washington if everybody communicated like this guy," said Harris.

***

Crawford was never sure when or how the Silent Deacon left the room. He remembers wiping his eyes which were burning from the latent nicotine, ammonia, and urine which formed a toxic cloud that hung above the Mothers room. When he regained his vision, the Silent Deacon was gone. It's like he had walked through the walls or sank through the floor. Harris was busy making notes on his tablet, and Janice was constantly adjusting her skirt to hide the coffee stain. Neither of them noticed the Silent Deacon leave.

"He left this for you," said Mrs. Robinson.

She handed Crawford an envelope.

"What's this?" asked Crawford.

"I don't know. Deak just put it in my hand."

"Then how do you know it's for me?"

"Because he was looking at you when he gave it to me."

"Then why wouldn't he just hand it to me?"

"I don't know why ole Deak does what he does," said Mrs. Robinson while emitting a blast of harsh smelling cigarette smoke out the corner of her mouth.

"Let's get out of here," said Janice. "I need to go and change."

"Yea," said Harris. "I think I have the picture here. Look forward to seeing you on Sunday Mrs. Robinson. It should be exciting for you and your Mom. Make sure you have a camera with you."

"Yes. I can't believe the President is coming here to see Momma. Lord, I just hope she's up to it."

***

Crawford saw the malignant son of Mrs. Robinson leaning against his car. He was smoking a Philly cigar and drinking something out of a bottle obscured by a paper bag.

Harris walked past the man like he didn't exist.

"Great," thought Crawford, who felt his fate sealing.

Janice walked up to the drooling monster and said, "Yo, you gotta move, we gotta go."

The son leered at her, belched loudly, held the thin cigar out toward her, and said, "You wanna hit?"

Janice leered back over the top of her designer sunglasses and said, "I don't have time for this."

"You need to make time baby. That little punk ass niggah boy you wit don't know how to handle your stallion ass like I do. Ain't that right Rev."

Janice looked at Crawford, sighed, and said, "Just get in the car and start it up."

Crawford didn't hesitate. He walked briskly to the driver's side and used his key fob to unlock all four doors and unlatch the lid of the trunk which bounced up and down like a yo-yo. He tossed his briefcase into the trunk and slammed it closed. This startled the son causing him to drop the bottle onto the ground. It shattered, its contents spraying up onto Janice's skirt and down her legs.

"Aw maaaaan!" screamed Janice. "I cannot believe this. What do you fools have against Egyptian cotton?"

"Ain't nothing baby. Let me lick the wine off them long legs of yours."

Janice quietly muttered, "Y'all gonna make me lose my mind."

"Damn baby, you already got some brown mess on your skirt, so I don't know why you're so mad."

Janice stood staring at him, mouthing something profane, almost growling.

The man, now laughing hysterically, moved away from the car, and staggered toward the house saying something about Janice being a "sloppy bitch". It was hard to tell because he was talking with the Philly stuck in his mouth of missing and rotten teeth.

Janice sat down in the car and said, "Drive. Don't say a mother loving thing, just drive."

15

The Will

Janice reclined her seatback to its limit which offered Crawford a view of her long legs, one of which was glistening with the sticky glow of Red Dagger wine (known colloquially as "Stab") a sickly-sweet concoction favored by teenage hoodlums and hopeless alcoholics. It was the grandson's wine of choice. They rode in silence. Janice's only action was to kick off her shoes and flex her exquisitely pedicured toes.

The day was proving to be another glistening monument in Crawford's pantheon of lousy days. Despite having endured yet another embarrassing encounter with the grandson, Crawford wasn't feeling shame and awkward humiliation. Instead, he was experiencing a heady feeling of accomplishment and a sense of confidence about what was going to happen next. The Mother had - in a way - agreed to appear at the CST for the Presidential visit, and he could claim credit for that. And then there was Janice.

He was intrigued by the way she handled that crude loathsome grandson and attracted to the blended aromas of cheap wine and hazelnut coffee. He liked the way she reclined next to him looking stately and serene. It wasn't such a bad day after all.

When Crawford arrived at Janice's home she remained still, her eyes closed, as if she was meditating, embracing the silence. He took the opportunity to look at her, examine her really, from her yellow head to lime-colored toes. He thought, "Am I supposed to say something? What's the protocol here?"

He jabbed her lightly on her shoulder with his index finger.

Her huge fake eyelashes fluttered like black butterflies, and she said, "Enjoying the view?"

To appear nonchalant, or at least less like a leering freak, Crawford had averted his gaze after poking her in the shoulder, but apparently, his gaze had lingered.

She returned her seatback to its full upright position and exited the car saying, "I need 10 minutes. You want to come up or wait in the car."

Crawford, imagining the grandson staggering behind them like a Zombie in hot pursuit of human flesh, said, "I'd better come in."

He followed Janice up the steps toward her front door. She was barefoot, with her giant heeled shoes stuffed into her handbag.

As he walked, he felt the envelope that the Silent Deacon had given him popping out of his inside breast pocket.

Janice walked into the bedroom of her apartment leaving Crawford to find a seat on her wicker furniture - a fan back chair that was overloaded with zebra skin pillows, and a love seat that looked old and brittle. Everything in the place was draped in Kente cloth, and huge peacock feathers bloomed from every vase. There were carvings of sub-Saharan beasts lined up on the coffee table, and a large painting of an African village dominated one wall. Crawford decided to sit on the small stool that at least had the benefit of a velvet cushion. When he squatted down onto the stool the letter made another appearance, stabbing him under the chin. He leaned his back against the wall and began to read the contents of the Silent Deacon's envelope.

There was a small note attached to the document. Crawford read the note first:

Dear Sir,

Mother Maude has taken a vow of silence. She will not speak, except to me, and I do not speak, except to God. Mother has vowed never to return to St. Stephens until it returns to itself. I, her brother in Christ, will tell her all she needs to know about the spiritual condition of what used to be her church.

Crawford then read the typed document:

> *And Jesus went into the temple of God, and cast out all them that sold and bought in the temple, and overthrew the tables of the moneychangers, and the seats of them that sold doves, 13And said unto them, It is written, My house shall be called the house of prayer, but ye have made it a den of thieves.*
>
> (Matthew 21:13)

Last Will and Testament
Mother Maude Cleary

This here is my last will and testimony. I lay here bound of my volition, restrained by chains of my choosing, incarcerated not by the force of man-made laws but by a sacred trust between me and the God I serve. I have given everything I have: my money, what little there is of it, my time, my talent -- what little I was born with, everything. Nothing remains for my children, or their children, nothing they want anyway.

Who the Lord sets free is free indeed! When the Lord sees fit to set me free, I will live out my parole with the knowledge that I did my time, and earned my freedom, a freedom that no man can take away.

You are probably thinking, "Why does that old woman want to leave anything to them stiff-necked people who stole her church, took her ministry, and drove the Spirit out of the Lord's House?" To you I ask this question: can I get my freedom with a heart filled with hate? I do not think so. I do not ask anything from these people. All I want is to bless them. I offer up a prayer that He will come again, yes, the second coming of our King. I pray that people of faith will rise and welcome Him and worship Him in Spirit and Truth, and that their church will be saved and that the people of God will be saved.

This is my last will and my last testimony.

Signed
Maude Cleary
Mother of the late St. Stephens African Baptist Church

Crawford thought, "She only speaks to the Silent Deacon, and he only speaks to God."

He re-read the will and said aloud, "She only speaks to the Silent Deacon, and he only speaks to God."

Crawford was fixated on the will, so he didn't notice that Janice had returned to the living room.

"What did you say?" she asked.

"She only speaks to the Silent Deacon, and he only speaks to God."

Janice rolled her eyes as she took the documents from Crawford and sat down on the fan backed wicker chair that made her look like an exotic model in a Malt Liquor advertisement.

She handed the letter and will back to Crawford.

"Well?" asked Crawford.

"So, help me understand," she began. She loved using the phrase "help me understand" which she had learned from Celestine. "The old lady only talks to that man?"

"Yes, the Silent Deacon."

"Everybody talks about the Silent Deacon, but I've never seen the brother."

"Yes, you have, we were just with him in the Mother's room. He gave me this note and her will."

Janice shrugged and said, "It doesn't sound like we're going to get anything out of that old woman. And what's with all that hocus pocus about the spiritual condition of the church and us being a den of thieves and having stiff necks. Who does she think she is throwing shade like that? Seriously? I mean really?"

Janice had changed into a short tight-fitting skirt and an equally alluring sleeveless blouse. The scent of lilacs, which matched her light purple hair, was toying with Crawford's concentration. He let the subject of the Mother's righteous and undoubtedly justified, indignation drop.

"Sorry I didn't offer you anything," said Janice. "It's just that I had to wash that nasty wine off."

"Yes, I understand. You smell much better now," said Crawford. "We'd better be getting back to the CST. I'm not sure what to make of this visit now that I've read the documents that the Silent Deacon gave me."

" Silent Deacon didn't give you anything. Mrs. Robinson gave you the envelope."

"True but this definitely was not written by Mrs. Robinson and she indicated that it came from the deacon.

"If I were you, I'd lose the letter," said Janice. "It's not helpful. They said they were coming to the service so that's all anyone needs to know."

Crawford knew Janice had a point, but he couldn't just act like the letter didn't exist.

16

The Debriefing

Janice bounced in her seat, joyously gyrating to Beyoncé's version of *Before I Let Go*. He wasn't sure if it was the vision of a six-foot woman dancing in her seat under a light purple wig or Frankie Beverly's funky melody, but the combination of sights and sounds put him at ease. It gave him something to think about instead of the interrogation he was sure to endure at the hands of Bearman. Despite Janice's distraction, he was still overtaken by the sweaty palms and feeling of nausea he endured whenever he entered The CST parking lot.

They arrived to find Bearman, Barbados, and Celestine glaring at each other, "So much for my mellow mood," he thought.

"Bout time you brought your behinds back here," said Bearman. "How did it go with the old woman? Is she coming or am I going to have to fit you for a wig and a house dress?"

Bearman didn't like hearing bad news. He had a sign from the Broadway musical "The Wiz" hanging in his office which stated in the gothic script:

"I Don't Want to Hear No Bad News"

Outside his office door hung an engraved wooden shingle that read:

"BEWARE: I kill messengers!"

This sign bore a drawing of a pirate and flag flying the skull and crossbones.

Crawford looked at Janice whose smirk was telling him to take her advice and just say, "Yes, she'll be there."

Crawford glanced at Barbados whose face offered no comfort, and then he saw Janice whispering into Celestine's ear.

"I'm really not sure," said Crawford. "I mean I was sure, but then the Silent Deacon gave me these documents, and now I'm not so sure."

"The who?" asked Bearman before snatching the envelope out of Crawford's hand.

He then turned to Janice. "I thought I told you to keep an eye on this fool. What is he talking about?"

Janice rolled her eyes and said, "I don't know. He claims some disappearing deacon gave him the old lady's Will. It's just a lot of nonsense about you being a thief and Reverend

Barbados having a stiff neck. Just some crazy mess about the old church. She's an old phony if you ask me."

Barbados laughed and while pointing at Janice's hair, which under the fluorescent lighting looked electric blue, said "So, you don't grasp the irony of you calling this old saint a phony?"

Janice rolled her eyes and made a ticking sound with her tongue hitting the roof of her mouth.

***

Bearman mumbled "What the fa…" repeatedly as he read the note and the will. He handed both to Barbados who was forced to share the copy with Celestine.

Bearman asked, "Who is this dude?"

"He is the Silent Deacon," replied Crawford.

"I think he's the old gentleman who used to be your father's armor-bearer. He'd carry his Bible, help him into his robe, make sure he had water, that kind of stuff," said Barbados.

"Lord," said Bearman. "Is that fool still haunting the church?"

"He is still around," replied Crawford. "And he was at the meeting at the Mother's house with the special agent."

"Aw no," said Bearman. "I ain't seen that fool in years. What about you Rev.?"

In truth, Barbados had seen the Silent Deacon every time he rose to preach at the CST. He sat in a far corner of the building, near a fire exit that led to the prayer grotto. But the truth does not always align with the facts, so Barbados was never sure if he was being visited by the real Silent Deacon or some apparition brought on by the stress of dealing with Celestine who only wanted him to hype her latest venture, or Bearman who only wanted him to pitch his latest fundraising scheme.

All Barbados knew was that as he'd start to preach, he would see the man thought to be the Silent Deacon, and then when he lost his resolve and forgot his message the man would seemingly disappear if he had ever been there.

"I don't know. I may have seen him, but maybe not," said Barbados.

"That's helpful," said Bearman.

"What about you Celestine? You see everything and everybody."

"I have no idea who you are talking about, and what's more I could care less. According to this note, this man doesn't speak to anyone but God so I don't see how he is going to tell this old woman anything."

"Good point," said Bearman.

"He writes," said Barbados, brandishing the note allegedly written by the Silent Deacon. "What if he writes and tells the Mother that the church or the CST is not worthy?"

"That old woman is blind as a bat," said Janice.

"It may be telepathic or through prayer. Clearly, he has some way of communicating with her, said Crawford. "He seems to have a way of getting through."

Celestine had heard enough "I don't think this creepy old man exists at all and if he does so what. From what Janice tells me, that old woman is in no condition to come to the CST. So, please, help me understand how we are allowing ourselves to be at the mercy of a bedridden woman who speaks to an invisible man. I mean seriously."

"She is in pretty bad shape," said Crawford, "but if the Silent Deacon advises her to attend church, I believe she will.

Bearman whipped out his iPhone and called Major Mosono Waago. "Got a job for you."

17

The Grotto

The grotto was accessible either from the emergency exit in the main auditorium or from the Pastor's office. It was built to be a serene sanctuary, set aside for prayer, meditation, and reflection. It quietly honored the late Reverend Bearman whose bust stood sentry just off the gravel path that led to his monument and crypt. Despite its lofty purpose, the place had become overgrown with a wildly disorganized array of weeds that had burst through disintegrating planter boxes and clay pots. The bronze likeness of the reverend had oxidized revealing green splotches that were partially obscured by white streaks of bird droppings. The birdbath was tilted at an angle; its basin having been reduced to serving as a giant ashtray for cigar butts floating in a brown fluid that repelled all living things. Only the bench that sat opposite the Reverend's grave seemed to have benefited from maintenance.

Barbados had direct access to the Grotto but he never so much as looked at it. He kept his blinds closed, and blocked the door leading outside with a chair filled with dust-covered books and outdated copies of *Christianity Today*.

There was no evidence that anyone used the grotto for its intended purpose. Unless you counted Huggey who took leisurely breaks to smoke cigars and toss the butt into the rancid birth-bath.

Barbados sat at his desk contemplating the one word that sat regally on the throne of his subconscious. He wondered how the presidential visit would launch his full-throttle *Escape* from the CST. "This is what I need to catch somebody's eye. Maybe Obama can hip me to a gig at a progressive think tank or a regular guest spot on CNN or MSNBC."

He looked up from his contemplations to see Crawford standing at the window bending the slats of the blinds so that he could peer out onto the grotto. The sight made him unexpectedly angry.

"That garden is in serious need of a reno, Pastor. Isn't that where Reverend Bearman is buried?"

"Huh?" replied Barbados.

"Reverend Bearman. Isn't he buried out there in the Grotto?"

"Yes. He's out there. Probably rolling over in his grave." Barbados continued. "What are your plans for after the big Obama visit?"

Crawford looked down at his feet, and up at the ceiling.

Barbados shook his head and said, "I guess I've failed you as a mentor."

"Well," replied Crawford. "I've been so busy searching for the Mother that I haven't had time to think about much else. I know that Hug, I mean Mr. Bearman has me working a table in the lobby during the Obama visit, but beyond that I…"

"A table?" said Barbados. "He's got you selling life insurance during the single biggest church service in our history. He's going to rob you of your chance to rub shoulders with Obama. And you're good with that?

"I'll just be there to catch people as they come in and out. He thinks it will be a great opportunity to grow my business."

"Your business?" Barbados wanted to smack Crawford across the face. "He's using you. If I were you, I wouldn't show up. But I guess you must. Huggey might need to put you in a wig and a housecoat if that old woman of yours doesn't show."

"Oh, she'll show up if the Silent Deacon tells her to," said Crawford.

"Really? You sound certain. You should tell me where he is so that I can be certain too."

"Actually, I have no idea," replied Crawford. "He's somewhat of a mystic. It's like he can get inside of your head and understand your thoughts, maybe even suggest thoughts."

Barbados felt his anger rising. "You've spent too many late nights watching sci-fi flicks. You should have been out trying to find a woman."

Barbados rose from his seat, suppressing an urge to put his hands around Crawford's neck and shake the bull crap that had obviously taken up residence in his well-barbered head. Instead, he put his arms around Crawford's shoulders and said, "We've really got to find that old man before Huggey finds him and makes him think we're running some kind of whore house."

"I doubt that Mr. Bearman or anyone else can influence what that Deacon tells the old lady."

"You think you've got this figured out, don't you?" asked Barbados. "But it sounds to me like you found a corpse who only communicates with a mute. You don't get it. Dudes like Huggey don't care about mystical old deacons and old church mothers. He cares about money, and he will do what he needs to do to get what he thinks he has coming to him. But none of that matters. You need to do what I tell you to do. Namely, find that old deacon and bring him in here. You may not be thinking about how to escape this zoo but I damn sure am. Son, this is no place for guys like us, we have a mission, a ministry to perform. This place is nothing but an updated minstrel show. Huggey wants us to dance around like Stepin Fetchit, and Amos and Andy. Celestine is nothing but a new age Sapphire with a mean streak. So, what are we gonna do?"

Barbados poked him hard on the shoulder.

"What we gonna do?"

He poked him harder.

"What we gonna do?

Crawford dodged the next poke fearing it would knock his shoulder out of joint.

"We're gonna find the Silent Deacon," said Crawford.

"My man!" said Barbados, hugging Crawford.

***

Huggey Bearman's office was dark, except for a yellowish glow that illuminated a small shrine he had set up in homage to his heroes: Father Divine, Daddy Grace, Reverend Ike, and his latest heartthrob Donald Trump whose Apprentice era photograph he had clipped from a copy of TV Guide.

Bearman was attempting to ward off the beginning stages of a migraine headache which was starting somewhere deep inside his frontal lobe and migrating out toward his eardrums laying waste to all physical sensations except for screeching pain and nausea.

Bearman had spent most of the week figuring out ways to capitalize on the Presidential visit. He enlisted

Teeny who shared his passion for promotion if not his cannibalistic avarice. Things were coming together nicely. He had already sold-out seats in the cry rooms – which he had converted to VIP seating (with bottle service) - at $500 a pop. He toyed with the idea of asking Janice to don a string bikini and work as a waitress but Teeny thought that might be too much. Other than that, the two meshed in their go big or go home attitude toward marketing.

The first 10 rows of the sanctuary were reserved seating. Fork over $1000 bucks and you'd stand a pretty good chance at being up close and personal with the Prez. General Admission tickets were going rapidly at $25. With no band to pay, no expensive speaker fees, not much in terms of expenses, he expected to net $100,000. Between the money and the presence of Teeny, he was in a constant state of arousal. The increased blood pressure was undoubtedly the cause of his migraine.

He grabbed two giant Advil tablets and tossed them back with a snort of whisky. This was all washed down with a lukewarm swallow of stale coffee sipped from an encrusted Krispy Kream mug. He poured another shot of whiskey into the mug and took another sip, grimacing from the bitter taste of coffee and cheap booze.

"I need you to find the Silent Deacon and bring that no talking son of a bitch to me before he tells Mother more than I need her to know."

"I'll find him," replied Mosono Waago, "But don't you think it is best if I conduct the interrogation. I have experience with this kind of work."

"Interrogation?"

"Yes. I know how to make people talk," said the Major.

"I don't need him to talk fool, I just need to keep him away from the Mother until after the service. What's wrong with you?"

"If you do not want me to break him then why are we looking for him?"

Bearman's migraine was beginning to cast its spell over the left and right hemispheres of his brain causing Mosono Waago to blur and fade into the darkness, then reappear as nothing but two red glowing eyes.

Bearman pinched the top portion of his nose and took several deep breaths. "Just find the old man and bring him here. Tell him that the old Pastor's son needs him to come and lay hands on him."

"But Barbados has no son."

"Not Barbados, I'm talking about the *old* Pastor, my father."

Mosono Waago stared at Bearman before saying, "But your father is late, why would…" Then he got it. "Ah yes, I see. Very clever sir. Very clever. This is a ruse to get the old man to agree to come to you."

"You're a freaking genius, Major. Go find him quick before my head pops off."

***

Celestine was despondent. She had spent her time putting the finishing touches on a live-streamed talk show which was apparently going to be without its only guest, Michelle Obama. Despite countless inquiries, she had not received confirmation that Mrs. Obama would be accompanying the President on his visit to the Cathedral. In fact, if Janice was correct, the entire visit hinged on whether a dangerous lunatic could convince a moribund zombie that it was ok to visit the church. It galled her that, once again her plans were being destroyed by men - crude, imbecilic - men.

Teeny, not sensing the mood in the room, stated, "This thing is gonna be fire. I mean we're selling everything from buttons to broomsticks with Obama's face on it. We got a VIP room with freaking bottle service. I'm selling ad space in the souvenir programs, so every cent hits the bottom line. People go crazy over this kind of stuff. Imagine if he was still in office, oh - my - god. This is like that time I opened for Drake down in Austin at South by Southwest. Remember that. Fools were lined up three days in advance. I tell you – I love this stuff. When this is over, we've got to get back into the business. Celestine, I'm telling you we have got to take this thing National, Hell, Global.

Ordinarily, Celestine would have been glad to ride the wave of euphoria that Teeny was generating as she prowled the room like a boxer warming up before the main event. Instead, she found it difficult to not see Teeny for what she was, a muscle-bound man masquerading as a well-toned woman. That had always been Teeny's problem since she transitioned. When she got excited, like she was now, she took on a certain mannishness that irritated Celestine. The strutting, the pounding of her fist into the palm of her hand, and the annoying tendency to throw imaginary punches.

"She isn't coming," said Celestine.

"Who? The old lady? Huggey has that handled," said Teeny who was now bobbing and weaving like Marvin Hagler in a mini skirt.

"No, Mrs. Obama, and please stop moving around like that."

"She's got to come," said Teeny. "We've scheduled a chat and chew immediately following the service. Just before your live-streamed interview. I've got tickets sold already."

"For the interview?" asked Celestine.

"For everything baby," growled Teeny.

"Well, it isn't going to be. I've heard directly from Mrs. Obama's staff that she will not be accompanying her husband. Something about seeing her daughter perform in a school play. Ridiculous. Besides, Crawford came back with a weird letter from that spooky old Mother. It seems she takes spiritual advice from that pervert who hangs around the church. Why would a so-called Mother need to take direction from a man, any man, especially a creepy little man who preys on women?

Teeny was imagining cartoon dollar signs melting into pools of excrement. "Wait so we can still make something of this. We've dealt with no- show acts before. Remember when Black Eyed Peas didn't make it to Cincinnati, or how about when Big and Rich got stranded outside St. Paul in a blizzard. The show must go on baby, you know that."

"This show," said Celestine, "is dead on arrival. That old woman is too old and sick to go anywhere. Janice has seen her. This whole event will probably get us arrested for running a swindle. But it will be worth it to see them take Barbados and your man Huggey to jail."

"You know I'm not into men like that," said Teeny.

"I know you're not, but I just like saying it. By the way, does Huggey know about your little situation down there?" said Celestine while looking at Teeny below the waist.

"He doesn't have a clue, poor thing."

Celestine smiled slightly; her mood has improved.

18

The Deacon Speaks

Huggey laid on his office floor with his eyes closed entertaining visions of himself and Teeny luxuriating on a Tahitian beach. Teeny was glistening with suntan oil that made her muscles look razor-sharp and defined, ready to explode beyond the confines of her string bikini. Huggey felt that muscles looked good on a woman and Teeny had the physique of a world-class bodybuilder – at least that's how she looked in his imagination. His relationship with Janice was a farce. She was a stallion, but she really wasn't his kind of female. Too thin, too pretty. He liked Teeny's hard little face and loved the way she walked with that little manly swagger and the way she talked with that rough, husky voice. Huggey was savoring a Jack Daniels, neat, booze sliding down his throat carrying away the effects of the migraine that was still tearing at his brain.

Hearing someone enter the room, he opened his eyes and saw the huge sweaty head of Major Mosono Waago looming over him. "I have located the deacon," whispered the Major.

"Help me up," said Huggey, who upon rising felt unsteady and nauseous.

Mosono Waago ushered him toward a desktop computer set up on a small cart in the corner of the office.

The monitor was split into four squares, each showing an image of an obscure portion of the building. Mosono Waago was obsessed with keeping an all-knowing eye on areas he considered covert hideouts for people he believed were a threat. It was never fully understood who these people were, or why they were hiding in the building, or who they were hiding from. He had cameras installed in broom closets, utility rooms, and oddly, the meat locker in the cafeteria, which proved useless because the lens was perpetually frozen over. The Major paged through endless images of stairways, shelving, interior walkways, crawl spaces, and utility rooms until he came to a set showing the four executive offices. All the CST staffers, being hopeless paranoids, knew that either Huggey or Mosono Waago were spying on them and rarely said anything of consequence while in the office. Barbados thought he had figured out where the camera was hidden in his office and took pleasure in glaring at a particular spot in the room while mouthing obscenities and tossing up his middle finger.

Huggey looked at each sector and all he saw were a series of pilotless desks and otherwise empty rooms. "What am I supposed to be looking at?" he asked.

"The Pastor's office. Look through the window that looks out into the Grotto. Don't you see him?"

The blinds for the window looking out onto the Grotto had been raised providing a hazy view of the dilapidated garden that held the remains of his father. He liked to go out there and relax, collect his thoughts, and maybe smoke a cigar. He hadn't been out there in months because the place had become so nasty. He left it that way to spite Barbados who he knew wouldn't sit out in that overgrown rat-infested graveyard, who would. But clearly, even through the lens of the security camera, he could see the back of a man who was sitting there looking at his father's grave. The man wore a black suit and a fedora. There was something about the rounded shoulders, the slump, the downcast angel of the hat, the white hair showing just under the brim. It was his father's old confidante, the Silent Deacon.

"What are we sitting here for?" said Huggey. "Go and get him."

"I cannot," said Mosono Waago.

"Why not."

"Because the only way into the Grotto is from the emergency door of the auditorium – which just now, is locked.

"You're the head of security. You've got to have a key." Said Huggey.

"Yes," said Mosono Waago.

"Well?"

"That is just it. I have a key but apparently, the lock has been changed."

"Dang," said Huggey. "Wait, we can go in through Barbados's office."

"Of course," said Mosono Waago. "There is just one issue with that. His office is also quite locked, and he has also taken the precaution of changing the lock on his door. So, you see my situation."

"We've got to get in that Grotto even if I have to bust a door open. Follow me."

They walked briskly through the building, with Huggey making one stop to gag and vomit in the men's bathroom. As they crossed through the lobby, he cursed the skylight which was allowing ultraviolet rays to blast through his aviators, temporarily blinding him to the point where he had to grab Mosono Waago by the elbow to keep from falling over.

They arrived at the waiting area of Barbados's office to find it unlocked. Barbados's door was open although the lights were off and the blinds looking out into the Grotto were shut and lowered to the floor. The door leading to the Grotto was propped open by an unused copy of the yellow pages.

Huggey went out into the Grotto and stormed past the bust of his father to the bench that oversaw the old man's gravesite.

There was no one there.

"We've been played," said Huggey. "The old dude is playing with my head." He staggered to the bench and sat down, listing to one side.

***

The Grotto was a grotesquely uncomfortable place to spend the night. It had the macabre feel of the set from *Night of the Living Dead*. No one would camp out in this place unless they had a burning desire to be decapitated with a chainsaw or have their flesh ripped apart by cannibalistic creatures from outer space. Unfortunately, Crawford had been ordered to maintain a vigil in this God-forsaken place by Barbados who had a hunch that the Silent Deacon would make a nocturnal appearance. Crawford leaned against the door that provided emergency egress from the auditorium. That way he could slip into the place if he was being surrounded by a gang of long-toothed rats. The darkened auditorium was spooky too, but at least it was clean.

He also figured this was as good a place as any to nab the Silent Deacon since the elusive little man had only been seen at the altar or in the Grotto. No one knew where he lived, or where he parked his car. Actually, no one was even sure he owned a car or a house. Then there was Janice who ridiculed him for searching for a man who – in her head - did not exist. "What is with that girl," thought Crawford. "She was in the same room with the man earlier that day and yet she swears not to have seen him."

Crawford was becoming irritated with himself for being the fall guy for every bully and moron in the universe. He thought about Barbados bullying him into going on a vain and senseless hunt for the Silent Deacon, and then about the idiot grandson who threw his iPhone into the dog yard. "What is with these people," he wondered. "What is with me?" His entire life had been based on people poking at him and snatching his belongings. "It's like I have a sign on my back: Kick My Ass!" It was at this moment that the emergency door punched him firmly in the butt.

Normally the perpetrator would have been Huggey Bearman who made a habit out of barging into places. But this time the actor was a small man in a black suit and fedora.

Crawford muttered, "Oh, excuse me, sir."

The Silent Deacon looked at him with pursed lips and a quick squint of the eyes – a sign Crawford took as thinly muted disgust.

The deacon walked past him, doffed his fedora at the bust of Rev. Bearman, and made his way to the bench. He turned and glared at Crawford and patted the space next to him on the bench.

***

The Silent Deacon was exhausted, having spent the entire day locking and unlocking every door in the facility. He had not actually changed any of the locks. He simply exchanged one for another, successfully creating confusion and frustration. He had sat with his back to every hidden camera in the building, causing Major Mosono Waago to make mad dashes in attempts to capture him. The truth was that he had spent much of the day in Huggey's office, watching the son of his Pastor lay on the floor trying to overcome the headaches that had bedeviled him since he was a child. It had been a full day, but he had exhausted Huggey and his accomplice. They had given up trying to find him and were now simply hoping that the Mother would show up at church the next morning. She would, of course, he really had no control over that. It was just the natural order of things.

This boy beside him was not ready for the task he would soon be asked to perform, but again, he had no control over who was called, he was only a messenger.

The boy was sitting next to him, his head down, staring at his hands like he was a child who had committed an infraction and had been called before the school principal. The boy was learned and diligent, but he was also vain and lacked the courage he would need.

The Silent Deacon removed a folded sheet of paper from the inside pocket of his jacket. It was an old-style church bulletin, the kind that had been typed onto mimeograph paper and printed using an ancient machine like the one locked in the bowels of the building. The program was weathered with age and the type was smudged but legible. The deacon handed the folded program to Crawford without looking at him.

19

Ready or Not

Crawford examined the folded program with the eyes of an archaeologist, reveling in his find of a papyrus fragment but aware that the slightest touch would turn its fibers into dust before he could read the ancient text. He wanted to open it and dive headlong into the inscrutability of the Silent Deacon. He was hoping for something profound, but despite his intense curiosity, he could not summon the strength of spirit required to unfold the document, let alone read it. He didn't feel morally equipped to grasp its mysteries. So, he sat allowing his focus to evaporate into his surroundings, which had become cold and moist, filled with scraping and rustling sounds coming from dark corners.

Crawford was an aficionado of the dark images generated by the motion picture industry. He believed that this grotto, like any grotto, was inhabited by rodents, a hideous clan of flesh-eaters slithering around, angling to trap him and feed on his body. "Solenodons," he thought. Crawford had written a screenplay for a science fiction thriller based on a small vicious rodent native to the island of Hispaniola. It's working title was "Solenodon!". The long-nosed rat-like creature fascinated him because no other mammal, except perhaps Celestine Nash, could inject venom with every bite. Unfortunately, the solenodon was a klutz, the clown prince of rodents. When frightened, it would look around with its sinister eyes before lowering its head to the ground as though by faking blind ignorance it would become invisible to predators. If it was really in a jam it would run, and after a few comic steps trip over its own clown shoe feet until it just rolled. Not an effective way to escape cats, dogs, or the occasional mongoose. This idiotic trait is driving the solenodon to extinction and unfortunately makes it laughable as an exotic supervillain. Too bad because it does inject venom from its teeth.

Crawford, at some point, realized that the Silent Deacon had left – or disappeared. Crawford slipped the folded program into his inside breast pocket where it would be safe until he gave it to Barbados as an unsuitable but convenient substitute for the Silent Deacon.

Crawford re-entered the auditorium finding Teeny and Janice hard at work instructing a crew on how to divide the seats into various levels of sponsorship.

"VIP Silver seating is over here," said Janice pointing to a section near the front but off to the side.

"Right," said Teeny, "And the Gold seats are just in front of them. Seven rows. And remember, the platinum seats should have bottled water and a mint on each seat."

A light crew was busy programming the lights and sound based on cues that Teeny had provided. Soft amber light for the prelude, electric blue for the entry, and processional which was to be conducted while *Hail to the Chief* played from the speakers.

"Do you still play that for former Presidents?" asked Crawford.

"Damn Skippy," said Teeny. "What the hell else would we play."

"Maybe a processional hymn?" said Crawford, "Like What a Fellowship" or "Onward Christian Soldiers."

"Come get your fool," Teeny said to Janice.

"How does he get to be *My* Fool", asked Janice.

"Uh-huh," said Teeny with the knowing grace of a woman who knew. "Just get him. He's getting on my last nerve."

"What have you been up to out there?" asked Janice.

Crawford, feeling a rare sense of pride and accomplishment, said, "I've been meeting with the Silent Deacon."

"Ha, yeah, right." laughed Teeny.

"You mean your imaginary man from earlier today?" asked Janice. "Or have you been talking to Deacon Rush? Or is there really a difference?"

"No. I've been with the Silent Deacon. He's given me a message."

"What?" asked Teeny.

"A message. He handed me a document that…" Crawford remembered that he had no idea what the document said.

Whatever good vibe he felt was replaced by the realization that Barbados was waiting out there for him to present the Silent Deacon. He was not waiting for another bizarre document, he wanted to talk to the man himself, the genuine Silent Deacon of myth and legend. It would be useless to try and disabuse Barbados from the impractical idea that he could convince the old mystic into convincing the Mother of the Church to greet President Obama. Crawford had become convinced that the deacon was not only real but more than real. He was like The Shadow of radio suspense and comic book lore; whose powers of invisibility and mind control were beyond the bounds of human experience. Barbados was no match for a reincarnated superhero "who knew where evil lurked in a man's heart". Crawford was unable to figure out how he would explain all of this to Barbados. All that he could do was offer him the document that he was afraid to read.

He selected Reverend Barbados's cell phone number, hoping to get a busy signal. Barbados answered immediately, "Talk to me."

"Yes, this is Crawford, sir. I have news for you."

"I know who it is, son. Keep him there. I'll be there in five minutes." With that Barbados disconnected the call.

"Sir, sir," said Crawford in a futile attempt to explain himself.

The program shifted in his pocket as he sat on a folding chair behind a table that had been set up for the next day's festivities.

The placard attached to the front of the draped table read "SOUL TOUCH BEAUTY PRODUCTS". The table across the lobby read "BEARMAN FUNERAL HOME". Next to that was "LEGACY OF HOPE" the table to which he would serve his exile while his friends and fellow churchmen were meeting a historic President of the United States. One booth had a spinning wheel where the dial would land on financial service. Spin to Win: Health Insurance, Life Insurance, Mutual Funds, IRAs, a cornucopia of services concocted by financial planners. The brilliance here is that you really wouldn't win anything other than a brochure with a broad meaningless description of the plan. People loved to play, even if what they won was worthless. There was one booth outfitted as a complete barbering stall, and another set up as a shoeshine stand, the lobby had the look and feel of a county fair.

A SECOND COMING

Major Mosono Waago was having a spirited debate with a vendor over the placement of his booth, and Celestine was busy reviewing the 4-color souvenir brochure that was set to be sold for $25 apiece. It occurred to Crawford that no president, not even the current Commander in Chief, would succumb to this level of commercialism. But it was all going to happen, and he would have a ringside seat for the most grandiose debacle in the history of the modern promotion.

Barbados came through the front doors of the lobby looking uncharacteristically casual in a training suit and tennis shoes.

"I just came from a quick workout," he said. "I like to unwind before sitting down to make final edits on my sermon for tomorrow."

"Yes, I'm looking forward to that," said Crawford.

"So, where is he?" asked Barbados.

"I don't know," said Crawford.

"What's that now?"

"I don't know where the Silent Deacon is. I was with him in the Grotto, but he slipped out on me."

"He what?" said Barbados smelling like Grey Flannel cologne.

"We were talking together, and he gave me a message and then he just kind of disappeared."

Barbados glared at him and took a menacing step closer. "A message. He talked to you?"

"No," said Crawford, "He didn't say anything, but he gave me a document."

"Another damn document. What's this one, *your* last will and testament?"

Crawford reached into his pocket, pulled out the folded pamphlet, and handed it to Barbados.

20

The Program

Barbados was a professional minister who should have understood the implications of the document that he held in his hands. Yet he flipped the document from front to back, opened it briefly, and then squinted down at the front page as if it were incomprehensible.

The front of the small pamphlet revealed a black and white photographic portrait of a middle-aged woman who sat majestically under a large ornate hat. She looked serious and commanding, glaring at the camera with a piercing glare. It was a look that said, "I am clearly a woman of substance, and you?" The corners of her mouth were slightly upturned giving the impression that she had a smile hidden somewhere. Perhaps her intimidating glare was an act, or maybe not. Above the photograph was the heading "In Memory", and beneath were the words "Sunrise, July 2, 1921 – Sunset, The Time is Now".

Barbados shoved the pamphlet under Crawford's nose and said, "What is this?"

"It looks like a funeral program," said Crawford, then almost to himself, "Why would he give me a funeral program?"

"I know what the Hell it is," said Barbados, "but what does it mean 'The Time is Now'? I've never seen that on a funeral program. That's not a date, it's a threat."

Barbados began to read the inside front cover of the program which told the story of a woman born in Clarendon County, South Carolina the daughter of Cleotis and Mary Cleary. It described how she was a 1943 graduate of Allen University who spent her early career teaching primary school in Sumter. It went on to explain that she was married to Billy Mack Robinson who died in Europe during World War II, and how she moved north to establish a shelter for battered, homeless, and abused women.

"Fascinating obit," said Barbados, "But who is this Cleary lady and why am I sitting here reading about her and not conversing with the Deacon."

Crawford recalled the name Cleary from the will, and Robinson – from visits to the Robinson household.

"I believe Mrs. Cleary is our church mother," explained Crawford. I suppose she went back to her maiden name after her husband died during the War."

Barbados was beginning to suspect that Crawford was a double agent, working for both Bearman and the Silent Deacon. He inexplicably wanted to poke the handsome young preacher in the eyes – Three Stooges style – fingers spread apart, quick jab.

"So again, what does this," he was now waving the bulletin in Crawford's face, "have to do with me meeting the Silent Deacon?"

"This," said Crawford, "gently batting the paper away from his nose. "I'm not sure what it has to do with anything. I actually have not read it."

Barbados smashed the program into Crawford's chest and muttered a jumble of words, that seemed to contain some combination of "weird and nerd". Crawford let the offending document glide from his chest to the floor before bending cautiously to pick it up, prepared to fend off an attack from Barbados who had stepped back as if he was winding up for a kick.

Barbados may have kicked him in the head. Crawford could not focus on the words on the page which seemed to float haphazardly, doing a do-si-do across the page.

"I can't read this," said Crawford.

"What's wrong with you?" Barbados snatched the paper from Crawford. He began to read the Order of Service:

- **Musical Prelude**
- **Introduction / Words of Welcome   - Deacon**

- **Prayers – Deacon**
- **Scripture Readings**
  - **Old Testament – Rev. Crawford**
  - **New Testament – Rev. Crawford**
- **Musical Selections/Hymns**
- **Formal Reading of Obituary – Janice McCrae**
- **Eulogy/Life Tribute – Rev. Crawford**
- **Brief Informal Tributes**
- **Final Viewing of Deceased – The Family**
- **Closing/Benediction – Rev. Crawford**

"No wonder you can't read this. Celestine has you doing the whole funeral. She probably has you serving food during the repast too. You're going to be a busy man," said Barbados. "You'd better have your stuff together for this one. When is the funeral?"

Crawford pointed to the date printed on the top of the page trying to avoid telling Barbados that the funeral was scheduled for the next day, which was of course the same day and the same place as the Presidential visit. It also spared him from articulating the truth that the woman who the President was coming to visit was being funeralized on the same day. He decided to let these things reveal themselves.

But Barbados needed help. "Who did you say this woman was?"

Crawford cleared his throat before saying, "I believe Ms. Cleary is the Mother of the Church. I believe she is the woman that President Obama is coming to honor. I suppose this is all shockingly inconvenient."

Barbados went through the full set of emotional stages encountered by people facing disaster. First, he considered the pain and guilt at having been associated with reprobates like Celestine Nash and Huggey Bearman. Then he felt the anger at having to deal with a moron like Crawford and the frustration of having to negotiate with the Silent Deacon who was impossible to bargain with because he seemed to lead an imaginary existence.

At this point, he could see no upward turn, no reconstruction, or working through the problem on his way to acceptance and hope. He read and re-read the bulletin, checked his watch, glared at Crawford, and finally sat back on the rented folding chair, and closed his eyes.

***

Crawford took the bulletin from Barbados, who was now staring straight ahead as though in a stupor.

The words on the page had settled down and assembled themselves into reasonable sentences and paragraphs. He read slowly.

It was clear that Mrs. Cleary, wife, mother, women's advocate, caretaker of the needy, provider for the homeless, and encourager of the desolate, this mother of the church, lover of the Lord, and grandmother to an incoherent, drooling idiot, had passed away. She would not be meeting the President or anyone else on this side of the Jordan, but was, perhaps even now, enjoying a late snack in heaven.

If the Order of Service was correct, he would be responsible for eulogizing a woman who he had never actually met. What could he say about her? From his experience, he could only commend her for having lain neatly in her bed and for having a love of hymns, but that last part was hearsay.

The only other staffer on the program was Janice, who if he recollected properly, never attended funerals because they were unpleasant reminders that someone had died.

But there it was, perfectly typewritten and printed on a classic mimeograph machine. It could, of course, be a cruel hoax. No one would disrespect a former president of the United States by arriving dead. Even more ridiculous was asking an inexperienced minister to give the eulogy and then schedule an apathetic woman to read the acknowledgments.

He saw Janice now, helping Teeny move a folding table into position in front of boxes marked "Souvenir Programs". He knew he should probably tell her about her role but decided to call the Robinsons to verify the recent passing of their mother.

"Hi Reverend," said Mrs. Robinson sounding uncharacteristically upbeat. "The Deacon told me to expect your call".

"Yes well, yes. I just want to make sure you are set for tomorrow."

"It's been real sudden Reverend. She was doing fine when you were here. Just still and quiet. And then she just sat up in bed and held her arms up and shouted, 'I'm ready Lord.' That was it. She was gone. Just like that."

"Just like that," said Crawford.

"Yes, my momma's gone."

"I truly am sorry. If there is anything, we can do…"

Crawford felt ridiculous as he uttered the words because there was nothing on earth, he wanted to do less than get involved with Mrs. Robinson and her son, but he was running on minister autopilot, uttering platitudes, and making promises he had no intention of keeping.

"Well, we are just thankful that you will do the eulogy for us and that we can do the funeral at the church with the president there and all. That's a lot to ask."

"Well," said Crawford. "I would think that perhaps you'd want to maybe pick another day for your mother's homegoing. I mean this is all short notice like you said."

"No," said Mrs. Robinson, "The deacon showed us the bulletin. He must think this is best, so that's what Mother would want. Besides, she was planning to come to church anyway."

"Yes, but the chances of her meeting President Obama are should I say, somewhat diminished due to her being deceased."

"Yes, but you saw her. She wasn't hitting on much when she was alive. The Deacon gave me a card from the Bearman Funeral Home. We'll be ready in the morning when they come to pick us up."

Crawford wanted to say something comforting but all he could envision was the President showing up to be greeted by a corpse, sitting in a rocking chair in front of the auditorium. Much like the Mother in *Psycho* – Hitchcock's 1960 horror/thriller.

Mrs. Robinson took advantage of Crawford's silence to tell him that she was pleased he was doing the eulogy since he was the only one from the church who really knew Mother Cleary.

Crawford wanted to cry out that he didn't know her, but he realized that in a grim pastoral sense we did know her. He had prayed a meaningless prayer over her dying body, and he had been bullied and humiliated by her grandson. That made him almost like family. As the call ended, he knew that he was going to bear the burden of being her voice. He would speak the words for her historic response to the presidential honor.

Huggey Bearman lumbered across the lobby like *The Thing from Another World*, 1951. Huggey was bent at the waist as he lurched forward, each step threatening to send him headfirst into the floor. His suit was rumpled, and his hat was smashed straight down on his head so that the brim touched the top of his sunglasses. He managed to make his way up to Crawford who rose and helped seat him into an inadequate folding chair.

"Barbados is mumbling like a fool about some damn funeral that you set up. What the Hell are you trying to pull on me."

Crawford handed him the bulletin and stepped aside hoping to disappear into the crowd of workmen setting up a red-carpeted catwalk that Obama would use as a walkway into the auditorium.

Bearman pushed his hat upon his forehead in the style of a cowboy taking a break on a hot day. He then removed his sunglasses revealing two watering slits where his eyes should have been. He blinked several times and then began to read the funeral program. "What is this?" asked Bearman. He continued reading and finally returned his sunglasses to their rightful place, and said, "Not today, not right now! You all are not going to ruin this for me. I see what you are doing. Trying to score, trying to be a player. I'm the only player here partner and you and that mute are not going to mess this up. Major! I got something for you."

Bearman rose to his feet and staggered off toward Mosono Waago who was still in heated negotiations with a vendor. He held the bulletin in one fist, stopped, ripped it into several pieces, and then threw the shreds into the air like confetti. He then turned and yelled back at Crawford, "I'm the only damned player up in here, understand?"

Barbados, having recovered from the shock of the mother's death, intercepted Bearman, had a brief conversation with him, and then came up to Crawford.

"Don't worry son," said Barbados in a Show Must Go On manner. "I know what is going on and I've got this. We know you didn't plan this funeral and put your name down as the eulogist. But you gotta face the facts, Son. If the old lady is dead, and I'm not sure she is, there certainly is not going to be a funeral here tomorrow. Not for her. Not for anyone. You understand that right?" Barbados did not wait for an answer but continued, "Good. You need to get those people on the phone and let them know that you are sorry for their loss, but nothing can be done for them until maybe Monday or Tuesday." Barbados put his hand on Crawford's shoulder and gave it a firm squeeze.

"I've already called the family, sir"

"Great, then it's settled. I knew there wouldn't be an issue."

"Well, there isn't an issue, except that the family has a firm commitment from Mr. Bearman to have the funeral tomorrow. At least they are being picked up in the morning by the Bearman Funeral Home."

"Impossible," said Barbados.

Crawford shrugged.

"You mean to tell me Bearman's people are picking up the family?"

"Yes, and the family is very appreciative."

Barbados made a show of putting his hands to his head and then covering his eyes. He muttered vaguely to himself and then, as if hit with a thunderbolt of clarity said, "Oh my goodness Crawford, don't you understand." He turned quickly in the general direction where he had conversed with Bearman, who had left the area with the Major.

"There is no way that family will ever see the inside of this church," said Barbados, not unless you are there with them when his people show up."

"Of course," said Crawford, who had now become resigned to the certainty of being murdered by either Huggey, or the Grandson, or the Major, or now Barbados, who was ending the conversation by placing his hands on both of Crawford's shoulders and shaking him violently.

21

Darwood, Who Art Thou?

Crawford spent most of the night pouring over a huge photo album that chronicled the life and times of Mother Maude Cleary. The album, bearing the title "Keepsakes" in chipped and faded gold script, was bound by a cord weaved through two holes drilled into the left edge of the book. The front and back covers were made of thick plastic-coated cardboard that was sturdy enough to line the walls of a bomb shelter. The ravages of time had caused the edges of the cover to split and fray, with one edge held together by black electrical tape. The pages of the album were made of black construction paper which had turned gray with deterioration. The glue holding the photos to each page had dried allowing the photographs to either drift freely through the album or become semi-attached to the page by ancient strips of transparent tape. Maude Cleary's life's work had thus become a random image loosely confined in a volume of memories that no one remembered.

Crawford examined a picture that, according to Mrs. Robinson, was baby Maude. The black and white image was out of focus and fading, but it still revealed a small child staring bewilderedly into the camera. She was completely enveloped by a huge white gown, with her tiny bald head propped up by a pillow making her look strangely like the old woman he had prayed for several days earlier. There was another photograph of a farm family gathered proudly in front of a dilapidated shack that was most likely their home.

There was a picture of Maude as a school-aged child, standing proudly with two other girls, wearing her church dress, looking clean, but patched up and careworn. There was yet another picture of girls seated on steps outside the shack, hair in ribbons, faces looking bright and hopeful. There was a headshot of a man in military attire which had become detached from the page and had drifted into the spine of the album. He was smiling broadly, his military hat cocked at a jaunty angle, the collar of his shirt too big for his narrow teenage neck. He looked too young to shave, almost like a child dressed up in a soldier's uniform.

Another strip of pictures was from a photo booth, a boy and girl grinning into the camera, heads touching, faces ablaze with silly grins and Vaseline. The pictures were randomly displayed, having been jostled, removed, and haphazardly re-inserted. But if you went through the book carefully it told a story

Crawford went through the book with Mrs. Robinson seated beside him, explaining the meaning and vintage of each picture. One photograph, taken with something called a Polaroid camera, showed a stout little boy standing proudly at a church lectern.

"Who is this stately young man," said Crawford. "He's pretty sharp."

"That's Darwood," said Mrs. Robinson. "He's sitting right over there."

Crawford looked at the older version of the chubby little boy in the picture whose name was Darwood Robinson, not by whatever ghetto pseudonym his friends used on the street.

"Darwood?" asked Crawford.

"He wasn't always like this," said his mother glancing over at her son who was sleeping fitfully in a recliner.

"Darwood?" said Crawford.

Crawford found it hard to reconcile the brute who had tossed his phone into a deranged dog's yard with the pleasant looking boy named Darwood who looked like he was speaking before a church. "How," he thought, "do you go from nice chubby little Darwood to the snoring Cossack in the reclining chair." It was a question that he'd have to put on hold.

There were dozens of pictures of sad and tired women, and other pictures of the same woman looking vital and confident. Before and after shots of some kind. There were no names or dates, just picture after picture of women showing the extremities of their existence.

"So many women," said Mrs. Robinson. "She helped so many women. She called all of the ladies even though they came to her all broken and beaten. Some of them were drunk or drugged up, and some of them were hustling their bodies, but she would call them Miss or Mrs., and would treat them like ladies."

Mother Maude had operated her shelter out of a four-story mansion that had once been owned by a clothing manufacturer. The clothing baron's warehouse famously caught fire in the early 1900s causing the deaths of hundreds of girls who toiled in his shops. Local legend told that the ghosts of these children migrated to the home of their old boss and held nightly ragers during which they tossed silverware in the air, rattled chandeliers, slammed doors, and raised havoc with the internal plumbing. Their spectral hijinks eventually drove the industry giant, his wife, and four daughters out of the place, but not before he made a public spectacle by standing outside his stately manor waving his cane while yelling, "Don't you little mongrels try to follow us. We're done with you." Despite the damping effect, this had on the local real estate market, he managed to sell the property to an unsuspecting industrialist. Years of urban decline and white flight finally did what the ghosts could not, turning the old mansion into a haunted house. Local youth enhanced the legend by setting fire to the place each year on the night before Halloween. It became a vacant burnt-out eyesore inhabited by crack addicts and poltergeists until Mother Maude acquired it from the city for payment of back taxes. She used donated materials and labor supplied by frantic women fleeing domestic violence to renovate the building. Hanging drywall and replacing windows and doors that gave these women confidence and dignity. It also enabled them to build a haven.

"Whatever happened to the old mansion?" asked Crawford.

"Reverend Bearman's son took it," said Mrs. Robinson.

"Took it?" asked Crawford.

"Yea, Mother bought the house with old Reverend Bearman. Mother didn't have much money and Rev. supplied most of it. He was supposed to put the deed in Mother's name but never did. So, when old Rev. died his son found out that his Dad owned the place. They put the ladies out and he put his funeral home in."

"Until recently I didn't even know that Mr. Bearman had a funeral home," said Crawford.

"He thinks he owns everything," said Janice who had just awoken from a nap,

"Well, that broke Mother's heart, having to move the Ladies out and having to move into this little place.

Darwood was a caretaker, doing odd jobs in that big old house. Something always needed to be done and it gave him a purpose. But there ain't nothing to do in this little place, and when Mother took sick, he just kinda went to pot."

"Who is Darwood?" asked Janice.

Crawford motioned to the man sleeping in the recliner with his mouth open, and his eyes darting around behind closed lids.

"Speaking of Mr. Bearman," said Crawford, "His people will be here in the morning to bring you all to the church."

"We'll be ready," said Mrs. Robinson.

Janice had managed to curl her lengthy frame onto the sofa and glanced at the photographs that had fallen from the photo album while dozing intermittently, continuing her on-again, off-again nap. At times, in a silent display of teamwork, Crawford would lift the album off his lap so that Janice could stretch her legs. Mother Maude's photos and letters were engrossing but were not enough to keep him from noticing the shape of Janice's thighs and calves, and the subtle lemony scent she gave off every time she moved.

Finally, she awoke fully and started to examine the photographs in detail. Although she could not claim to know any of the women in the photos, she had a feeling that she recognized their faces, like they were people she knew, but could not quite recall their names. Maybe it was their "look" or vibes that she knew. The bruised eye sockets and cheeks, the twisted and matted hair, and the cracked swollen lips of women who had been slapped around. She knew the tired look of a woman who spent all day wondering when her man would come home and all night wishing that he would go away. She knew the woman behind that face because she had lived with that woman, or a woman like her, until one day that woman just disappeared and left her in the care of the state.

There were pictures of children too. All of them thin and gaunt but with a glimmer of hope in their eyes. Mother Maude provided the first hot meal they had eaten in weeks and let them wash in a tub instead of the sink in a convenience store restroom. They would wear a clean pair of pajamas - a first for many of them - and luxuriate in warmth, before finally surrendering to sleep in a mother made bead.

"That will put hope in your eyes," said Janice to no one in particular.

"What?" asked Crawford.

"Nothing," said Janice.

"Mother used to say, nothing is ailing that child that a hot meal and a hot bath won't fix," said Mrs. Robinson.

Janice spread the photographs of the children and mothers on the coffee table. There were dozens, covering the table, then the floor under the table, and then migrating all around the sofa. Photograph after photograph of women finally enjoying safety and comfort, not knowing how long it would last, making the most of the time they had. Wondering if it was only a dream from which they would awaken to find themselves sleeping in the back seat of an abandoned car, or against the cold tiles of the subway platform.

Janice studied the face of each child as though she was searching for something or someone. None of the faces meant anything to her until she got to a picture of a tiny girl with a pinched face and sad droopy eyes. The girl's thumb was planted firmly in her mouth. "Look at them droopy eyes," she thought. "Droopy little eyes on a droopy little face. Take that thumb out your mouth droopy girl. Stop sucking that thumb or you'll have big buck teeth to go with those droopy sad eyes." She turned the picture over and tossed it into her bag.

***

Darwood was accustomed to sleeping upright like a horse, so he snored through all the talk and soft laughter. The room had quieted, and the silence jarred him awake. He saw Crawford asleep with the old photo album on his lap. His mother was no longer in the room, but that girl was there, sitting on the floor with her legs crossed, looking at the old photos that his mother should have thrown away years ago.

"The dead has arisen," said Janice.

"All closed eyes at sleep," said Darwood.

"Yours were."

"I was watching y'all. Waiting for that corny dude to pass out."

"Well, he's out."

"Huggey's boy Moso," said you had something for me."

"Yes, I got it."

Janice reached into her bag, pulled out a stack of bills, and handed it to Darryl.

"Hell yeah," said Darwood. "I can do some damage with this." He began thumbing through the stack pretending to count the money. "You need to come with me. It's time to scat. Ain't nothing here for a stallion like you."

"I got some things to tie up here first," said Janice. "Like maybe your Grandmother's funeral?"

"Huggey's boy said there wasn't gonna be no funeral."

"Not tomorrow, but probably later." She looked over at Crawford who seemed serene.

"Oh, I dig it. You strung out on his punk ass huh?"

Janice smirked but said nothing.

"Well, I paid my respects to Mother so forget that. I ain't gonna sit up in no service trying to kiss Obama's ass.

This here is my inheritance," he said waving the stack of cash, "and it's about to get lit like the fourth of July."

"Good for you dude," said Janice. She was thinking that he would drink and gamble the $10,000 stack of cash away in less than a week. Then he'd be back in that same recliner if Huggey didn't sell the house out from under his mother.

"So, you're just gonna leave your mother in the hands of Huggey and that crew. Damn, I knew you were cold but, damn," said Janice.

"My mom will be alright."

"Really? OK, I guess you know," said Janice.

"What are you talking about? Huggey knows if he messes with my momma…"

Janice put her hand up and said, "Huggey knows he bought you."

"Ain't nobody can buy me."

"Whatever. Take your money and go. Have a drink on your Grand mom's name. I'm sure Huggey will."

"Maybe I'll buy his ass a drink. Oh, and Bearman said that I could um, borrow the boy's little company car."

Darwood stood up, took Crawford's car keys off the coffee table, and slammed out of the house into the night air.

***

Darwood Robinson drove directly to the Camisole, an after-hours strip club. Major Mosono Waago was there seated ringside for a cage match featuring two overweight exotic dancers refereed by a teenage girl who should have been home getting rest for cheerleader tryouts at the local high school. Darwood came in flashing bills like he had just hit the lottery, which in a sense he had.

"My man," said the Major, "My big man. I see you got healthy tonight. I am happy for you. I will buy you a drink."

"Ain't nobody buying me nothing," said Darwood. "When I get paid everybody drinks on me!"

Darwood bought rounds for a small congregation of congratulatory deadbeats who sensed free ride. The group would have been larger, but the owner would not allow him to use the private VIP lounge figuring Darwood had robbed a convenience store and that a police raid was imminent.

"You are the man!" yelled Mosono Waago trying to be heard over chants of "Put her in the Vice" as one heavyweight lady wrestler put her smaller, shapelier opponents head between her tree trunk sized thighs. "See," continued the Major, "You are taking advantage of the opportunity. Let me give you some advice my friend. Do not let your emotions stop you from taking advantage of your opportunity."

"What are you talking about?" asked Darwood.

"Can I speak to you honestly?" asked Mosono Waago, who had leaned in close to Darwood just as the smaller woman managed to get to her feet, her head still between the giant thighs, and executed a flip so that the larger woman flopped down on her backside and then was quickly rolled onto her back. "You must take your money and go far away."

"Who is supposed to take care of my mother, and see that my grandmother gets her due?"

"Aw man," said the Major while slapping Darryl on his broad back. "Do not worry about that. Your grandmother is late. She is living with her ancestors. She is ok. You, that is who you must worry about now. You."

Darwood stared at the Major who had turned his attention to the match which had turned into more of a twerking contest between the teen referee and the slender wrestler who was celebrating her victory. The Major's head was beaded with sweat and he held a handful of singles up toward the women who twerked in front of him. The detective was so transfixed that he never noticed Darwood clumsily rummaging through his pockets and leaving the Camisole through a side door.

22

The Final Service

Crawford was caught in a surreal dream, surrounded by angry belligerent men seeking to be husbands and fathers but finding only frustration and financial regret. The faster they ran, the be hinder they got. Knee deep in the quicksand of a low paying job, grasping hopelessly to a five-dollar lottery ticket and a pint of brown liquor that almost made him forget until he remembered. Fighting the riptide current, drowning men attacking the only people who could guide them safely ashore. Floating above the chaos were a sea of black and white photographic faces of Mother Maude, and her lost ladies and their waifs all living in a gilded mansion.

After a moment of uncertainty, he realized that he was on Mrs. Robinson's living room sofa, under a quilt blanket surrounded by photographs, letters, and a half-consumed cup of tea. It was just after dawn. Janice, who had replaced the grandson in the recliner, was snoring softly under her quilt. She had removed her wig revealing intricate rows of black braids of silk forming the perfect crown for her sleep-softened face, unadorned by cosmetics and false eyelashes. "Why?" Crawford thought, "would anyone cover up hair like that?"

Crawford glanced at his watch and realized that it was time to get moving, change clothes, freshen up.

But his wristwatch, never one to lie about such things, told him that there wasn't much time for his normal ablutions. Huggey's funeral people would be there in an hour.

"Janice?" he said. She stirred, yawned, rubbed her eyes like a little girl being roused for school.

"What time is it?" she asked.

"It's about eight. If we get going, we can go home, change, and be at the CST to meet the family."

"We've met the family," said Janice, turning her back to him.

"No, I mean meet the family at the front of the church. You know, to escort them in."

Janice shrugged while Crawford searched for his keys. He looked on the coffee table and then patted himself down, before asking, "Have you seen my car keys?"

Janice thought for a second and said, "Darwood has them. He took the car."

"What?"

"He took your car, ok. He said something about Huggey giving it to him. I think he got paid off."

"So how are we supposed to…" Crawford took out his phone which had lost its power at some point during his long night of research. "Is your phone charged up, we need to call Uber or Lyft. We've got to get going."

Mrs. Robinson entered the room fully dressed in her Sunday attire. "Morning Rev."

"Good morning Mrs. Robinson. You're dressed early."

"Well, the funeral people will be here in about a half-hour, so I am not that early, I'm pretty much on time."

Despite being fully dressed and covered by a blanket that smelled like stale cigarette smoke, Crawford had enjoyed a good night's sleep. He felt calm and refreshed when he should have been panicking.

Janice disappeared into the bathroom and Crawford went through his options while sipping a Styrofoam cup of coffee and wolfing down a large slice of pound cake. He did not have a change of clothes, nor did he have a toothbrush, deodorant, or anything that would benefit a fastidious man who normally spent two hours getting ready. He did have a firm idea about what he would say about Mother Maude.

Janice reappeared in a blue skirt and a white blouse. Her braided hair was tied in a bun. She looked fresh and radiant. "I always keep an extra skirt and a top in my bag," she said by way of explanation.

Crawford thought of his thin briefcase which looked good but was only able to handle a couple of brochures and a knock-off Montblanc pen, both pathetically irrelevant at a time like this. A toothbrush, even a mint, and a razor would have been far more useful.

***

Darwood Robinson drove through the night with the seat of Crawford's car pushed back as far as it would go and reclined to a position that afforded him an excellent view of the top of the dashboard. He had just enough room to work the pedals and navigate the car which he did in manic jerks and swerves. "This ride is too small for a grown man," he thought. "I gotta swap it out for a man-sized ride as soon as I get a chance". He pulled recklessly into the driveway of The Bearman Funeral Home, stopping just short of the wrought iron gates which Huggey had added for security. He searched the massive set of keys that he had lifted from Major Mosono Waago until he found a round object with one grey button. He pressed the button, the gates swung open, and a series of lights came to life providing a lighted trail right up to the front door. He could have found his way in the dark since the mansion that had once been his home.

The outline of the place looked the same. The wide inviting front porch, and huge front doors seemed to be open twenty-four hours a day. Darwood tossed Crawford's keys into one of the big potted plants standing guard on either side of the front steps. He then walked along the side of the house toward the rear. Motion sensors caused the entire back of the house to light up revealing a camera that was attached to the top of the carriage house. Darwood gave it the finger, and then for extra measure relieved himself on the tarmac. A black hearse was parked in front of the carriage house sandwiched between a large sedan and a pickup truck with an extended rear cab. He had always wanted one of those.

Darwood tried the door to the carriage house, but it was locked. Then he went back to the mansion and tried a door marked Authorized Personnel Only. It too was locked. He started trying keys on the Major's cumbersome set which probably unlocked the doors of Bearman's entire empire. The weight and discomfort made carrying them impossible which is why Mosono Waago had tossed them on the bar top at the Camisole. There were at least 20 keys and clickers on the chain. Darwood never carried keys when he was the custodian at the mansion because Mother Maude never locked anything. The only intruders were ex-husbands and boyfriends who were drunk and clumsy. When they showed up it was better to just let them howl at the front door until the cops showed up and arrested them for breaking a restraining order. But Huggey locked every door to the place like somebody really wanted to break into a joint crowded with corpses. Finally, Darwood found the key that unlocked the big grey door leading inside. He turned on the lights and was confronted with a room full of caskets. Some were closed but most were open. The closed caskets were lined up at the door, probably waiting to be rolled out to a hearse. He opened the lead casket closest to the door and found an old guy looking back at him through eyes covered by sunglasses. "Who gets buried with shades on?" he thought. "Must be bright where he's going. Nice suit though. You look good my man." He looked down at his own attire, the greasy jeans, motheaten old t-shirt, and fatigue jacket that he had brought home from the military service. The sleeves were frayed and there were black splotches of oil on the front. He opened another casket and found a middle-aged woman dressed entirely in gold. The interior of the casket was gold, her blanket was gold, shoes were gold, and there was a gold hat laying off to her side. "That's just ignorant," thought Darwood, "I don't like that kind of show-boating. You ain't all that. All covered in gold like you got it like that. Take that mess off! Take it off!" The woman lay in silence. Darwood shrugged and closed the lid. He opened the lid of the next casket and was confronted with the withered face of his grandmother. She had once been a strong and forceful woman, running her mouth, getting on his nerves, throwing out his friends, and pouring his liquor and weed down the toilet. She helped broken women she didn't even know. But now she laid there, cold and gone forever. He looked down at her face and caught a glimpse of something, a flicker of an eye, maybe a curl of a lip. He reached into the casket and shook the old woman saying, "Mother?" She did not respond so he shook her again, crying out, "Momma, Momma. Don't ignore me now just because I had a little drink. I had to come over here to see you tonight because I don't know where I'll be in the morning, I ain't even sure one hundred percent where you'll be in the morning." He shook her again and got no response, "Damn. Well, I had to try it." The tears stung his eyes and rolled down his face. He removed the pink handkerchief that his grandmother held in her hands and asked, "You mind?". He then wiped his face and blew his nose. "I know, I know, you don't want it back."

Behind the caskets were several racks of clothing. Suits, hats, shoes. It looked like a discount clothing store. "They probably use this stuff to dress dead people," he thought. He rummaged through the racks until he got to the big and tall section. "Here we go, this gear is for the overweight stiffs." He removed his clothes and dressed in a black suit, white shirt, and a shiny pair of size 15 gunboats. "What the hell," he said, "I might as well meet the president too."

***

Crawford and Janice sat at the kitchen table. Janice reviewing the obituary and resolutions she was tasked with reading, and Crawford frantically scribbling notes for his eulogy. Mrs. Robinson caught them glancing up at each other and said, "You'd better watch it or there is gonna be a wedding after the funeral. Mother would love that."

Janice rolled her eyes and said, "Please."

"I've spent half my life watching women, I know what I'm talking about."

"Interesting," said Crawford.

"Right," said Janice.

"Funerals are a good place to meet people," said Mother Maude's caregiver who had arrived to ride with the family.

"Why?" asked Janice. "It seems really sad and depressing to me."

"No, she's right," said Mrs. Robinson. "See I…"

A truck horn blared several times and Crawford could hear what sounded like a madman stomping up the front steps. Janice tensed and jumped to her feet when they heard the front door open and slam against the wall.

Crawford peered through the small dining room into the living room where he saw Darwood, dressed in a humongous black suit and the largest pair of patent leather shoes he had ever seen. He was carrying a cardboard box holding four cups.

"Y'all ready to go," said Darwood. "I stopped and got coffee cause I figured we wouldn't have time on the way."

Everyone in the house stood looking at Darwood like he was a Cro-Magnon man who appeared unexpectedly in their living room. Crawford wasn't sure but it looked as though Darwood had shaved, or at minimum washed his face. His hair, normally a matted mass of dreadlocks was hidden under a shiny blue du-rag. No one said a word until Janice said, "Nice suit."

Outside was a tricked-out Chevy Silverado - with the extended cargo bed and a luxurious passenger cab. A casket, which hung at least a foot over the end of the cargo bed, was strapped down with rope and bungee cords and surrounded by flowers that had been stuffed between the sides of the casket and the truck.

"Let's roll," said Crawford, gathering photographs and stuffing them into the album. "You ready?" he asked as he handed the album to Janice.

23

Homegoing

Darwood, imagining himself in the video game version of *Fast and the Furious*, passed cars on their passenger side, swung back into their lane, and then stomping on his brakes to avoid rear-ending them. He muttered, "Get out my way fool" while aimlessly adjusting the temperature controls and tuning the radio, annoyingly finding stations that played nothing but static. He slowed at green lights and raced through stale yellow signals. He made luxuriously wide turns, adjusting his body as if the force of his body language could keep the truck from veering into the opposite lane. Crawford nearly bit through his lower lip as he clung tightly to the passenger door handle. He glanced back into the rear cab and saw the three women huddled together, united in terror, clutching one another as Darwood barreled through a stop sign at a busy intersection. Only Mother Maude managed to keep her composure.

Even the relief of arriving at the CST was spoiled when Darwood accelerated into the parking lot, scattering police officers and lot attendants.

"Park in the front," yelped Crawford.

Darwood acknowledged him by breaking hard causing everyone to lurch forward. The casket slammed into the back of the passenger cab, Mother Maude, at last, registering her disdain.

"Damn," yelled Janice. The truck grew quiet as everyone took inventory.

"OK," said Crawford. "Mrs. Robinson, why don't you sit tight while we get things prepared for you."

Mrs. Robinson's hat was tipped forward covering her eyes, in the style of a slumbering cowboy. Her hands were shaking as she rummaged through her purse in search of a cigarette.

Darwood exited the truck and began releasing and untying the nest of bungee cords that kept his grandmother from rolling onto the highway.

Major Mosono Waago ran from the building yelling, "What are you doing?"

"Taking my grandmama into the church, what does it look like I'm doing."

"No," said the Major, his eyes red and his huge head brimming with sweat. "No, you cannot do this thing."

Darwood gently rolled the casket down the ramp that had been stored under the cargo bed. Once down he unlatched and carefully raised the gurney.

Women were streaming onto the concourse from the surrounding community. They walked solemnly toward the building, mentally paging through memories while acknowledging each other with nods of vague recognition. One group clearly knew each other. They were dressed in oversized t-shirts with a stylized image of Mother Maude and graffiti words "One Love" above her portrait and "R.I.H." below. They were also wearing skin-tight jeans and red stiletto heels. Judging by their age they must have been part of Mother's last cohorts.

"You must stop," said the Major, who stood with his arms outstretched like he was holding back a crowd. "Do not disgrace your ancestors. Please, put her back on the truck. We had a deal. You do not want to do this thing." He pulled his jacket back revealing a holstered handgun.

Darwood glanced at Crawford and said, "Follow me," and began pushing the gurney toward Major Mosono Waago. Crawford put his right hand on the casket as though comforting the deceased, guiding her into the sanctuary for her last worship service.

Mosono Waago looked like an NFL nose tackle making a goal-line stand. He had a wide stance and a look of fierce determination on his face. Crawford glanced back to see Darwood bare what remained of his rotting teeth and heard him emit a low growl. Mosono Waago stood his ground, even held his palm out, before side-stepping nimbly out of the way, his hand still at his waist, looking like a fat matador.

"Uh huh," said Darwood, barely missing the Major's cowboy booted feet. Crawford shrugged and kept moving.

***

Janice observed a different scene playing out on the concourse. A procession of black Suburban SUVs rolled to a stop behind the pickup truck that had performed admirably as Mother Maude's hearse.

"I think you'd better check that out," said Janice drawing Mosono Waago's attention to the line of oversized vehicles.

"Do not tell me what to check. Can't you see that I am dealing with important things here? We are expecting the President."

Janice followed the Major over to Agent Harris who was standing near one of the SUVs.

"Hi Janice, good to see you again," said Harris.

Janice noticed that Harris was looking at her like she had a live snake wrapped around her neck. He kept glancing at her head and then glancing away. Men usually did that when she had selected a truly audacious hair color - like lemon-lime, or royal purple, or fire engine red. She had also caught them staring at her legs when she was wearing a ridiculously short skirt. Men did not like to be caught staring, she thought, except for Huggey who leered at women unrelentingly and dared them to say something about it. He once made a show of wiping slobber off his mouth while taking a long lustful look at a woman's breasts. When she voiced her disapproval he said, "You need to put those things away before you cause me to have a stroke." But Harris was not that kind of guy. He glanced at her again and said, "I must tell you that your hair looks great."

Janice patted herself on the head remembering that she had forgotten to don one of her straight waist-length wigs. She had decided to wear a raven black number, in keeping with the occasion. But there had been no time to stop for a hair change. This is the first time in months she was appearing with her hair uncovered and natural.

"New look? I mean it looks nice, but...never mind. It looks nice."

Harris turned to Major Mosono Waago and asked, "So has the Mother arrived. Mr. Obama would like a few words with her before they enter the sanctuary for the service."

The Major, looking ashen-faced and unsteady said, "She is late."

"Oh, ok. So what time are we expecting her."

"She is already here, she has been taken inside, unfortunately."

"Oh. Then I'd better inform the President. We'll just escort him to where she is and then he can do his thing. Hey, and that little fella you are always looking for? The quiet little man. He's with the President, so he can probably take us to the Mother."

"He is here?" said the Major. His eyes glistened as he patted his side. "Where is he, I need to speak to him immediately."

Harris looked at Janice who shrugged, then he looked back at the Major. "Let me get the President and we can all go see the Mother, OK." Then he whispered to Janice, "Is he ok?"

"Not especially," said Janice.

"The President cannot speak to the Mother," said the Major.

"But you said she was here?"

"She is here but she is late," said the Major.

Harris glanced at his watch and asked, "Where is she?"

"I do not know," said the Major. "I believe she is in the room where they take people who are..." The Major looked down at the ground.

Harris looked at the pickup truck that was loaded with flowers. He opened the passenger cab door and saw Mrs.

A SECOND COMING

Robinson and another lady sitting quietly. He closed the door, looked at Janice, and asked, "She's dead? What the Hell is going on?"

"We thought you'd been notified," said Janice, when in truth neither she nor Crawford had given any thought to President Obama's visit.

"No one told us anything," said Harris. "What's going on Major?"

" Nothing is going on," said the Major. "But I think we should get Mr. Obama inside. I have been wanting to meet him because like me he is from Africa."

"He's from Hawaii," said Harris, "and I thought you were from Cleveland."

Janice saw the President walking arm-in-arm with a little man in a shabby suit.

"I think the President got tired of waiting," said Janice.

***

Huggey was addressing a group of women in the sanctuary with Deacon Rush at his side. "Look, I don't know who told you that you could sit here, but y'all got to move."

"Unless you are family," interjected Deacon Rush, a placid grin concealing worry and regret.

"Shut up," said Huggey. "These *heffahs* are no kin to President Obama."

A stout woman sitting closest to Huggey hugged her purse - which was the size of rolling luggage - close to her chest, giving her a solid, immovable presence. Every woman on the row had a similar look of stern formidability. They were all wearing black or grey coats over dark-colored suits. They wore simple earrings and jewelry, and their application of cosmetics was reluctant, almost chaste. They gave off an aura of women who should not be trifled with. Deacon Rush picked up on it. Huggey plowed ahead, either unaware or choosing to ignore the signs.

"Look," said Huggey. "You are in other people's seats. People have paid to sit where you are sitting, and you have got to move. I'm asking y'all nice right now but in a minute, I am not going to be so nice."

One woman, wearing colorful African attire said loudly enough to be overheard, "I ain't got to move nowhere."

"Who is this fool?" asked another lady who had a careworn face and thick strong hands with haphazardly painted fingernails.

Other women arrived and squeezed into seats next to people that they knew, greeting each other with the quiet warmth of fellow mourners.

"They ain't doing no harm Huggey," said Deacon Rush. "Let them be."

Huggey glared at Deacon Rush and said in staccato fashion: "Shut-up - Negro - please. Please shut up. Go and get those people out of the seats over there. Make yourself less useless." Huggey was pointing to the section of the sanctuary that Teeny had marked for premium seating by placing bottled water and mints on each chair. A large group of women had crowded into the seats and were enjoying the treats while commenting on how Mother Maude always knew how to care for her ladies. Huggey grabbed the frail deacon by the shoulders and shoved him in their direction, causing the old man to stumble foolishly.

"That ain't right," said a woman while glaring up at Huggey.

"What ain't right is your fat ass sitting in a seat you didn't pay for," said Huggey. Now for the last time, I need all y'all to get the hell up and go to the balcony. That's if you got the twenty-five dollars to sit up there. If not, take your ass home. You can see this mess later, on YouTube."

Huggey never saw Mother Maude -- encased in wood and metal – rolling to the rescue. Darwood had given her a final push, allowing the slight slope of the auditorium to carry her down the aisle toward the altar. Crawford had lost the battle he was waging to keep the casket centered. It veered dangerously close to the pews on the right, brushing against whoever was sitting in the aisle seat. Deacon Rush saw the impending collision and spared Huggey from being crushed by muttering, "Oh Lord."

Huggey looked up in time to see the corpse-laden missile barreling toward him at ramming speed. He managed to wedge his huge frame into an area occupied by the solid woman who was using her magnificent purse as a chest protector and was not inclined to give him space he desperately needed. He stepped on her feet causing his ankles to roll, sending him sideways onto the floor where he was bombarded by feet clad in sensible shoes and an elephantine purse that was apparently loaded with lead bricks and horseshoes.

The casket was still on the move, the front edge clipping the side of a pew causing it to spin 180 degrees until the back of the casket slammed into another pew providing just enough force for the front half of the lid to pop open making the Mother Maude's final resting place look like the cab of a log flume ride. Crawford and Deacon Rush attempted to prevent the runaway casket from crashing into the altar but decided against it as the ornate box bounced off the first step of the altar, spun another 180 banging hard enough to slam the casket lid shut and immediately open. Crawford and Rush worked together to center the casket as if the whole event had been a planned dramatic entrance. They then helped arrange the flowers that had survived the crushing ride in the pickup truck. One spread of pink roses supported a sign that read "Mother Beloved" and held a photograph - between the words Mother and Beloved - of a woman who was clearly not Mother Maude. Darwood ripped the imposter's photo from the display which he then adjusted lovingly on a flower stand.

Mother Maude had shifted in the coffin to make it appear as though she was laying on her side.

"Why is she laying there like that?" asked Darwood. "She wasn't like that when I took her out of the funeral parlor."

Considering her rough arrival at the altar, Crawford said nothing.

"She looks fine," said Deacon Rush. "Almost like she's trying to get up and go on her way."

Darwood pushed her back into position and said, "That's better."

Women began to line up to pay their respects to the Late Mother of St. Stephens African Baptist Church. A few had obtained small photographs from a table in the lobby, which they placed carefully in the liner on the underside of the casket cover. They touched the withered and cold hands that had, at the low point in their lives, providing warmth, and strength, love, and self-worth.

Janice was still in the lobby, carefully arranging photographs from the album onto the vendor table that had been reserved for Legacy of Hope. Mrs. Robinson agreed to give away the pictures to anyone attending the funeral who could recognize themselves. There was no sign-in book for visiting mourners, but women stopped and looked through the photos before entering the sanctuary. "My God, look at me," said a woman as she gazed at a photograph of a thin morose looking specimen who bore her no resemblance.

"Oh Lord, is that my baby?" said another woman as she stared at a photograph of Mother Maude cradling an emaciated child who looked to be no more than 1 years old but was 3 or 4, her growth stunted by a life on the run. One by one they recognized their pictures and recognized each other. It had become a family reunion, filled with memories, laughter, and tears.

Six women in identical black outfits, each sporting wide-brimmed hats that completely obscured their faces, made their entrance ahead of The Bishop, spreading black rose petals as they walked down the aisle - in the left together, right together stride of a dignified procession. The Bishop was attired in an ornate clerical robe and a large conical hat, and he made his entrance like a monarch, grinning and waving at people who had no idea who he was. Behind them all was the 44th President of the United States walking arm-in-arm with a small man wearing a black fedora.

Seeing the procession, Crawford stood at the lectern and raised his arms, signaling everyone to stand. He watched as the women continued to enter, greeting Mrs.

Robinson and Darwood, who was still wearing the electric blue du-rag and was chewing noisily on a large wad of gum.

The Bishop took a seat next to Rev. Barbados who had slipped into one of the chairs in place behind the lectern. There was also a chair reserved for President Obama, but he had been led by the silent deacon to a seat close to the door that led to the Grotto.

"I will now offer a Word from the New Testament," began Crawford.

(Romans chapter 8 verses 35, and 37 to 39)

> *Who will separate us from the love of Christ? Will hardship, or distress, or persecution, or famine, or nakedness, or peril, or sword? No, in all these things we are more than conquerors through him who loved us.*
>
> *For I am convinced that neither death, nor life, nor angels, nor rulers, nor things present, nor things to come, nor powers, nor height, nor depth, nor anything else in all creation, will be able to separate us from the love of God in Christ Jesus our Lord.*

And, from the Old Testament, I will read (Isaiah chapter 57 verses 1 and 2.)"

> *The righteous perish, and no one takes it to heart; the devout are taken away, and no one understands that the righteous are taken away to be spared from evil.*
>
> *Those who walk uprightly enter into peace; they find rest as they lie in death."*

The beginning bars of Hail to the Chief began to play and were abruptly halted when Crawford made the slashing signal across his neck.

Crawford continued, "The family of Mrs. Maude Cleary, late Mother to what was once called St. Stephen's African Baptist Church, welcomes you to this, her homegoing service. The family especially wants to acknowledge the presence of the Bishop of the Secular Cathedrals of America, his eminence Bishop, and Entrepreneurial Apostle R. X. Sandman."

Bishop Sandman stood up and removed his giant hat, kissed it, and handed it to Rev. Barbados who appeared surprised and sat there holding the missile-shaped headgear.

Crawford went on, "We also want to welcome, with great admiration, the 44th President of the United States, Mr. Barack Obama."

The audience clapped loudly and there were several shouts of amen and hallelujah.

President Obama acknowledged the applause by nodding his head and waving.

"We know that the President came here today to honor Mother Maude. She truly anticipated meeting you sir with great pride, but alas, it was not to be. Your visit is not what you or I or the leadership of this church had in mind, but God had other ideas."

Obama nodded.

A SECOND COMING

We will now continue the service with the reading of the obituary by Janice McRae.

Janice rushed down the aisle carrying the remains of the photo album that had been picked bare by mourners. She climbed the few steps onto the altar and stood in front of the lectern that had just been vacated by Crawford who stood off to the side mouthing the words, "We gonna be alright." She nodded at him and said, "Until last night I didn't even really know what an obituary was. I'm still not sure. I was supposed to get a script on what to say, but I stuffed it in this album and now I can't find it." Janice put her head down and choked back tears.

"It's all right baby," someone yelled, "just speak from your heart."

Crawford came up beside her and said, "don't worry about the obituary. Just say what you need to say."

Janice looked up at Crawford and saw nothing but compassion. Then she looked out into the audience and saw women holding pictures and she said, "Mother Maude lived a life, didn't she? She took us in when we had no place to go, I mean no place. She fed us when we were hungry and clothed us when our clothes were wet and dirty. But most of all she gave us life, at least the beginnings of life. Many of us found pictures of who we were back then. Thank God we are not who we were. We're not running or hiding or stealing or giving up our bodies. I look at this picture of this little pinch-faced girl," she said holding her photo up. "And all I can say is thank God for Mother Maude. She helped this little girl when no one thought she was worth saving. That poor little girl no longer exists. But I want Mother Maude to take this picture with her so that when she meets up with God in heaven, she'll have something to show God. She can say, God, I saved this one little life."

Janice then left the lectern and placed her photograph neatly into the lining of the casket. Other women and small children came forward holding pictures and placing them in the casket before returning quietly to their seats.

At some point during this offering, the President whispered something to his small companion, gave a quick salute to Crawford, and slipped out of the auditorium and into the Grotto.

www.ingramcontent.com/pod-product-compliance
Lightning Source LLC
Chambersburg PA
CBHW031243290426
44109CB00012B/409